Praise for This Book

"A must-read book for all the stock option tax issues that challenge even the IRS. Provides employees, executives, and advisors with highly readable wisdom to profit from their equity compensation."
Bruce Brumberg, Editor-in-Chief, myStockOptions.com

"A very good overview of the tax and financial planning implications of stock options, written in a way that's useful to experts and understandable to those who are not."—*Corey Rosen, Executive Director, National Center for Employee Ownership*

"This book does a great job of explaining the rules so a participant can gain the most value from stock options while avoiding common mistakes and pitfalls."—*Gordon Rapkin, Executive Vice President, Chief Marketing Officer, Transcentive*

"A comprehensive information resource for employees, explaining as simply as possible the complexities of stock options."—*Debra Sherman, Foundation for Enterprise Development*

"Should be required reading for anybody receiving options as compensation."—*Roy Lewis, co-author, The Motley Fool's Investment Tax Guide*

> The Certified Equity Professional Institute has designated *Consider Your Options* as required reading for those seeking CEP Level I certification.

Praise for Our Web Site (fairmark.com)

"One of our favorite sites."—*Newsweek Magazine,*

"One of the top 50 financial web sites."—*Money Magazine*

"A good newsy site, easy to navigate and fun to read. Its explanations are crystal clear."—*The Boston Globe*

Also by the Author

Equity Compensation Strategies
A Guide for Professional Advisors

Capital Gains, Minimal Taxes
The Essential Guide for Investors and Traders

Go Roth!
Your Guide to the Roth IRA and Other Roth Accounts

That Thing Rich People Do
Required Reading for Investors

Consider Your Options

Get the Most from Your Equity Compensation

2014 Edition

Kaye A. Thomas

A Plain Language Guide from

FAIRMARK PRESS INC.

About the Author

Kaye Thomas has over 30 years of experience as a lawyer dealing with tax matters relating to business transactions, finance and compensation. Much of that experience is in advising companies on how to establish and maintain equity compensation arrangements, and individuals on how to manage those benefits.

He also gives talks to groups of option holders and offers seminars to help tax professionals and other financial advisors develop expertise in dealing with employee stock options and other forms of equity compensation. His book *Equity Compensation Strategies* is designed to be used as a reference and/or course of study by professionals offering advice in this area.

Kaye maintains a free web site called the *Tax Guide for Investors* at **www.fairmark.com**, providing news and hundreds of pages of plain language tax guidance. The web site also features a message board where Kaye and others respond to questions and comments from readers.

Kaye's law degree is from Harvard Law School, where he served on the *Harvard Law Review* and graduated *cum laude* in 1980.

About the 2014 Edition

This is the eighth edition of *Consider Your Options*. It has been updated to reflect tax legislation and other developments through October 30, 2013. Changes from the previous edition are substantial.

A new chapter provides guidance on income tax reporting, describing the various information returns you'll receive (from the familiar W-2 to the special forms sent to ESPP participants) and how to reflect that information on your income tax return. Another new chapter addresses the Medicare tax on net investment income, which took effect in 2013. Chapters dealing with employee stock purchase plans now cover nonqualified ESPPs as well as qualified plans.

Changes in tax rates for both ordinary income and long-term capital gain took effect in 2013. These changes, which are reflected throughout the book, may affect strategies, especially for incentive stock options. Various other updates, including recent IRS guidance on vesting and the 83b election, appear where appropriate.

Visit our web site at *Fairmark.com* for updates on this book or to post a question or comment on our message board.

Part I
Laying the Foundation

The Big Picture

Stock options offer an opportunity to build wealth while participating in your company's success. Smart choices can make a big difference in how much you get from your equity compensation.

THIS BOOK IS FOR PEOPLE who receive *equity compensation*—benefits that relate to their company's stock. It covers all aspects of these benefits: their value as part of your compensation package, the investment issues you need to understand, and the tax rules that apply. You can use it to develop your own strategies, or to understand and evaluate the recommendations you receive from an advisor. Either way, it will help you get the most from your equity compensation.

We'll cover all the popular forms of equity compensation, including restricted stock awards, restricted stock *units*, and employee stock purchase plans (ESPPs). Our main focus will be stock options, though. They're the most powerful form of equity compensation—and also the most complicated. The way you handle your stock options can have a lasting effect on your financial condition.

An opportunity to build wealth

Your equity compensation provides you with an investment in the company where you work. Like any other investment, it represents an opportunity to build wealth. You shouldn't expect the stock or options you receive from your company to eliminate the need to save and invest through retirement plans, college savings accounts and so forth, but they can make a healthy addition to your net worth. And in some ways, stock or options you receive from your company are *better* than other investments.

Equity compensation gives you a stake in your company's fortunes. It's one thing to watch an investment grow in value, and quite another to participate in the rewards of a success you helped create. Companies offer equity compensation partly because it builds teamwork and provides a kind of satisfaction you can't get from other investments.

Tax savings are another potential advantage. The results here depend on the kind of equity compensation you receive and the strategy you choose. In some situations you'll come out better than if you received cash compensation and used it to buy stock.

No instructions

They say money doesn't come with instructions, and the same can be said about stock options and other forms of equity compensation. Your company may explain the mechanics of exercising an option, but they can't tell you *when* to exercise, or how long to hold the stock. It's up to you, alone or with the help of an advisor, to select a strategy.

3

> If your company won't help you figure out the best strategy, it's for a good reason. Companies can get in big trouble when they start giving advice to employees about taxes and investing.

A sound strategy is essential when dealing with stock options. Options are investments on steroids. They can muscle their way ahead of other investments, building value much faster than shares of stock. Yet they can also leave you with a bad case of SDS: sudden disappearance syndrome. The value that builds up so fast can evaporate just as quickly. Meanwhile, you have to deal with tax rules that can be tricky, even for a professional.

This book is written in plain language so everyone who receives stock options can understand the key points. It starts at the beginning, so you don't need any advance knowledge of investing, stock options or taxation. Our goal is to help you handle your equity compensation for maximum advantage without taking undue risk.

Public and private companies

Throughout most of this book we assume you work for a company where the stock is *publicly traded.* That means people can buy and sell the stock through a stock broker, and you can look up the price of the stock in a newspaper or on the Internet. See Chapter 28 for information about special considerations that apply when you receive equity compensation from a closely held, or *pre-IPO* company.

Major issues

People who receive equity compensation often have to make important choices. Here are some of the decisions you may face:

- How should I evaluate my stock options? Are they worth enough so I should accept a job at this company—or stay here when I have another offer?

- How should I handle my other investments when I hold stock or options in my own company?

- When should I exercise my stock options? Given a choice of different methods, *how* should I exercise my stock options?

- If available, should I make the *section 83b election* to change
  - my tax treatment?

- How long should I hold my stock? Should I sell as soon as possible? Wait until I have a long-term capital gain? Hold on as long as possible?

All these decisions have three components. They involve investment choices, so you have to understand risk and return. They involve tax planning, so you need to know which tax strategies pay off. And they involve personal considerations based on your financial situation and personality. The decision that makes sense for one person isn't necessarily best for someone else. Your choices should be tailored to your own situation.

One question you might have at the outset is whether to get professional advice, or handle these issues on your own. The next chapter provides tips on working with an advisor—or working without one.

2

Option Advisors and You

Companies that offer stock options usually provide a standard disclaimer: check with a professional advisor before deciding on a course of action. Here are some tips on selecting and working with an advisor—and on how to proceed if you go it alone.

THIS BOOK IS DESIGNED to be authoritative, understandable, and reasonably complete. That doesn't mean you necessarily want to forgo the help of an advisor. There's no substitute for the experience and expertise of a qualified professional. Even if you normally feel comfortable doing your own financial planning, you should consider seeing an advisor if you run into some of the more technical issues, or if your stock or options become a big part of your net worth.

Someone could write an entire book on how to select a financial advisor. In fact, someone has, and I recommend it: *Getting Started in Finding A Financial Advisor*, by Chuck Jaffe. Here are some tips on the specific problems in hiring someone to help with your stock options, and also on handling these issues without help.

Option advisors

I use the term *option advisors* for professionals who provide advice to option holders. They can fall into two different categories. Some are tax professionals, and others are investment advisors. There are some advisors who are fully qualified in both areas, but they are a distinct minority.

That can lead to frustration. You need help finding a strategy that provides a good tax result without exposing you to too much investment risk. You may find a highly competent tax professional who says she can't help you with investment questions. So you call an investment advisor who seems really smart and he says he can evaluate investment risk and reward but can't give tax advice. Neither one can evaluate a stock option strategy from all angles.

> Before you pull your hair out and scream, try to remember these professionals are acting responsibly when they limit their practice to areas of genuine expertise.

If you can't find an option advisor who's qualified to help with both kinds of questions, the best thing to do is read this book thoroughly and decide whether you need more help on the tax issues or the investment issues. Then try to find someone who handles that kind of question. In either case, look for someone who has a fair amount of experience in handling stock options. This is an area where competent professionals who lack specific expertise can go wrong.

Tax professionals

Tax professionals don't necessarily have a professional designation, but many of them are enrolled agents (EAs) or certified public accountants (CPAs). Most enrolled agents acquire that designation by passing a rigorous exam administered by the IRS. The requirements to become a CPA, and to maintain that license, are even more rigorous, but some of those requirements deal with audit issues that are not related to taxation. You can find skilled professionals in both categories.

> A *registered tax return preparer* has satisfied basic requirements to prepare income tax returns but may have little or no training in the rules discussed in this book.

Tax pros deal with plenty of technicalities, but some of the rules for stock options are especially arcane. Not long ago, stock options were given almost exclusively to a relatively small number of top executives. Most tax professionals rarely encountered these rules, so stock options received little or no coverage in the courses and seminars attended by EAs and CPAs. For the same reason, the IRS has offered only the skimpiest guidance on the tax rules for equity compensation.

The situation has improved somewhat in recent years, but there are still plenty of pros who trip up when dealing with stock options even though they're competent in handling other kinds of tax issues. Far too often they make mistakes even when their only job is to prepare a tax return. That's a good indication they won't necessarily know how to plan a tax strategy for your stock options. Look for experience in handling equity compensation before you rely on the advice of a tax professional.

Investment advisors

I use the term *investment advisor* for people who provide advice on investment risk and return. They seem to be everywhere. Some are stockbrokers, and others work in the personal banking department or trust department where you have your checking account. Some work for insurance companies, and some are independent, or work for firms specifically formed to provide investment advice.

> The professionals we used to call stockbrokers are now often called *financial advisors* or *FAs*.

As in the case of tax professionals, investment advisors do not necessarily have a professional designation. Someone wanting to become a stockbroker must pass an exam, but you should be aware that it is possible to pass this exam with little or no knowledge of equity compensation. Some stockbrokers have studied the subject long and hard, and have the ability to provide excellent service in this area. Yet there are many others who know less about stock options than you will know when you finish reading this book.

> Organizations that can help you find a good financial advisor include the National Association of Personal Financial Advisors (napfa.org) and the Financial Planners Association (fpanet.org).

There are many certification programs for investment advisors. These programs establish educational and other requirements to acquire and maintain a professional designation. The best known program leads to the *Certified Financial Planner* designation. If your investment advisor has this designation, often indicated by the letters *CFP* after his or her name, you are dealing with a professional who has dedicated a great deal of time and effort to gaining a thorough grasp of the knowledge required to be a competent financial advisor.

The course of study for the CFP designation covers over a hundred topics, however, and only a tiny fraction of that curriculum deals with equity compensation. The CFP designation conveys a level of professionalism but does not imply expertise in handling stock options. Some advisors have told me that after obtaining this designation they still had to figure out on their own what strategies would work best for employee stock options.

> The bottom line is that you can't assume someone has the ability to provide advice on stock options merely because of a professional designation. You need someone with knowledge and experience in this particular area.

Training for advisors

Fairmark Press Inc., the company that publishes this book, also offers a training program for advisors. Based on a book called *Equity Compensation Strategies*, which is specifically designed for use as both a reference and a course of study, the program includes exams that can be used to demonstrate competence. Unlike the earlier (and now terminated) program maintained by National Board of Certified Option Advisors Inc., this program does *not* lead to certification of the participants, but advisors who have worked through the *Equity Compensation Strategies* course of study have shown a commitment to this area of practice and acquired a superior base of knowledge for handling stock options and related items.

> When looking for specialized advice in this area, ask whether the advisor has completed the *Equity Compensation Strategies* course of study.

Your advisor's compensation

There are many factors to consider when choosing a financial advisor. Naturally you want someone with knowledge and experience, good work habits and a personality that fits with yours. Beyond those essentials, it's important to understand how your advisor is paid, for two reasons. You need to know how much the advice is truly going to cost, and also whether your advisor has a financial interest in giving one kind of advice when another might suit you better.

Fee for service. Some advisors charge an hourly fee, or a fixed fee for a particular service. This arrangement is relatively easy to understand and usually does not create any bias on the part of your advisor. For this reason, "fee-only" advisors sometimes suggest that they provide the most objective advice. That's a good point, but not necessarily a decisive one. You may find that you get excellent service from an advisor who receives other forms of compensation.

Assets under management. Another way to compensate your advisor is by paying a fee based on the value of the assets the advisor manages for you. (Some advisors consider this type of compensation to be included in the phrase "fee-only.") Overall, an advisor who is compensated this way has your interests at heart: the advisor's compensation grows when your portfolio grows. There's one issue worth noting, though. As a general rule, your stock options don't count as part of your portfolio. The advisor doesn't earn anything on that part of your wealth until you exercise the options and put the stock (or sale proceeds) into the portfolio. If the advisor tells you to exercise your stock options, you might wonder whether the compensation arrangement influenced that advice.

Commissions. Sometimes the advisor's compensation is invisible. This is when it is most important for you to dig for the details. It may feel like a great arrangement, because you didn't have to reach into your pocket to pay for the advice. In reality, the advice can turn out to be more expensive than you imagined.

In some cases the advisor (or the advisor's firm) receives a sales commission for recommending a particular investment. For some items, such as annuities, the commissions can be quite high. If the investment isn't really suitable, the advisor has been enriched at your expense.

One form of sales commission for financial advisors is called a mutual fund *load*. This is a sales commission deducted from the amount you invest in the fund (or from the amount you receive when you cash out). There are many excellent mutual funds that do not charge a load, and some experts say you should never buy a load fund. I say there's nothing wrong with putting your money into a load fund—if you receive investment advice or other services that justify this cost.

For example, suppose you make a $400,000 profit from your stock options and turn it over to an advisor who puts all the money into mutual funds that charge a 5% load. The immediate result would be a $20,000 reduction in the value of your investments. In effect, you've just paid $20,000 for that advisor's services. He'd better be a darn good advisor, because there are plenty of professionals who would provide excellent advice for a much smaller fee.

On the other hand, suppose your advisor spent a lot of time reviewing your overall financial situation and working out a stock option strategy. You received first-rate service and ended up putting *some* of the money into a mutual fund that charged a $5,000 load. Depending on the circumstances, $5,000 might be a reasonable price for the services you received. The key is to know how much you're paying, and to understand that a mutual fund load takes money out of your pocket the same as if you paid cash to the advisor.

Other expenses. Finally, you need to be aware that stockbrokers often make more money when you pursue certain strategies that may not be in your best interest. Brokerage commissions are good for the broker, but frequent buying and selling is almost never a good idea for the customer. Similarly, margin lending is highly profitable for the broker, but margin borrowing is usually unwise for the customer. Fancy hedging strategies may produce handsome fees for the brokerage firm, even if the best way to manage risk might be simply to sell your shares.

> There are relatively few advisors who intentionally give bad advice to pad their wallets, but compensation arrangements can make it difficult for an advisor to be completely objective.

Working with an advisor

Once you've selected an advisor, you'll want to work with that person in the most effective way. Here are a few suggestions. First, try to present the advisor with complete, accurate, well organized information. You'll save time and money and have a better chance of receiving good advice. Second, don't be afraid to ask questions. You should always understand the reasons behind your advisor's recommendations. Third, make sure it's clear what actions you are to take, and what actions the advisor will take. Then follow up to make sure everything happened as planned. Never assume anything!

Working without an advisor

Some people don't want or need an advisor, or simply can't find one they like. Here are some tips for people in that category.

Know what you have. Make sure you have a clear understanding of what you have. How many shares of stock do you own? Are they vested? If not, when will they vest? When can you sell them? Are there other critical dates you need to track? How much gain or loss, and what *kind* of gain or loss, will you report on your tax return when you sell your shares?

If you hold stock options, you need to track down even more information. Some of it may be found in summaries provided by the company, while other answers may appear in the stock option agreement you received at the time of the grant.

- What kind of option is it? How many shares does it cover? What is the earliest date you can exercise the option? Does it become exercisable in stages?

- What do you need to do when you exercise the option? Can you borrow to exercise the option? Can you pay the exercise price using stock you already own?

- When will the option terminate? Can you exercise after your employment terminates? What if you die while holding the option?

Without a clear picture of your rights and obligations you may overlook valuable opportunities or make other costly mistakes. One of the simplest and most painful mistakes is to permit a stock option to expire (which makes it completely worthless) at a time when it could have been cashed in for thousands of dollars. Normally there's no way to recover from this surprisingly common event, which is known in the trade as a *stock option lapse*—in case you've ever wondered what the letters *SOL* stand for.

> Every year, countless option holders make this blunder. Don't let it happen to you!

Learn about planning. Become as knowledgeable as you can about the tax and investment aspects of your equity compensation. Read this book carefully, and keep an eye out for other good sources of information. If you have questions, visit our message board at Fairmark.com. Using the search function, you may find that your question has already been answered. If not, you can post your own message. We don't guarantee a response, and we don't guarantee that any response you get will be accurate, but most of the time you'll get helpful information. It's free, and unless you choose to reveal identifying information, it's anonymous.

Let your computer help. If you prepare your own tax return, use a software program or an online service for tax preparation. You're far less likely to make mistakes this way than if you do your return by hand. But don't expect the software to do all the thinking for you. For example, the software may not "know" you need to file Form 8801, even after you've entered all the information about your stock options. If you don't "tell" the software to prepare this form, you may miss out on the AMT credit.

Avoid overconfidence. You're a smart person and you'll be even smarter after reading this book. That doesn't make you an expert, especially in the area of investing. The most costly mistakes usually occur when option holders overestimate their ability to handle investment risk, a subject we'll discuss a little later.

3

On Being a Shareholder

Anyone who receives equity compensation should know the basics of buying, owning and selling stock, and be aware of restrictions that may prevent or delay a sale of shares.

SHARES OF STOCK REPRESENT OWNERSHIP of the company. If your company has a total of 50,000 shares and you hold 500 of them, you own 1% of the company. Large, publicly traded corporations have millions of shares, often with a total value in the billions of dollars, so your percentage ownership in that type of company is likely to be a tiny fraction of 1%. The basic principle still holds: as a shareholder, you're no longer just someone who works there. You're also an owner, someone who shares in the company's success.

Shareholders are the ultimate bosses of a corporation. They get to vote on major decisions, and they also elect the board of directors, who set the overall direction of the company and appoint the officers. Typically you receive proxy materials in the mail at least once a year, telling you what matters are up for a vote. You can go to the shareholders' meeting and vote there, but the proxy materials also provide a way for you to vote by mail, sort of like an absentee ballot.

> In a large company, your fraction of ownership is so small that you probably won't have much influence over the outcome of a vote, but reading the proxy materials can give you a better idea what's going on and make you feel more involved.

The opportunity to participate in "corporate democracy" may give you a warm, fuzzy feeling, but it won't put food on the table. The economic rewards of holding stock come from dividends and growth in value.

Dividends

Profitable corporations sometimes pay out part of their profits in the form of a cash distribution to the shareholders. These *dividends* may be paid regularly, four times a year (a "quarterly dividend"), but companies can also declare "special" dividends intended as a one-time event. It's up to the board of directors to determine how much dividend to pay, or whether to pay any at all.

It can be nice to receive dividends, but it's useful to understand that dividends don't make you richer. Investors include the value of the dividend in the amount they're willing to pay for the stock, until the *ex-dividend date.* That's the day when it's too late to buy the stock and receive the dividend. Beginning on that date, investors no longer include the value of the dividend in the stock price, so the overall value of the stock is smaller. A dividend converts part of a shareholder's wealth from stock into cash, without any overall increase or decrease in wealth.

If you hold a stock *option*, you won't receive dividends until you exercise the option and become a shareholder. We'll discuss dividends from restricted stock awards and restricted stock units later.

> A company that declares a special dividend may take steps, as Microsoft did in 2004, to protect the value of stock options and restricted stock units. Otherwise those benefits would decline in value when the dividend was paid.

Growth in value

Dividends are usually less important to a shareholder than *appreciation*, or growth in the value of the stock. Many companies pay no dividends at all, even though they produce handsome profits. Others pay dividends, but at a level that provides only a fraction of the overall return the shareholders are seeking. Companies work hard to make their stock value grow, because that's usually the main concern of their shareholders.

Stock value can decline, too, of course. Companies can lose part of their value or fail altogether. The long-term success of the stock market has made it a terrific place to invest, but it also exposes you to risk. That's a subject we'll deal with later in some detail.

Stock splits and stock dividends

Most companies like to keep their stock price within a range that makes it easy for ordinary investors to buy shares. When the stock price grows high enough, they may *split* the shares. If you're a shareholder, you end up with more shares, but at a lower price per share. Overall, the split doesn't affect the value of your holdings.

> ✱ **Example:** You held 100 shares worth $120 per share before the stock split three for one. After the split, you hold 300 shares worth $40 per share. The total value of your stock remains the same.

Companies nearly always make adjustments to protect option holders if there is a stock split. For example, in a two for one split, an option to buy 400 shares at $20 per share would turn into an option to buy 800 shares at $10 per share. You end up in exactly the same place, because the total amount you pay to exercise your option, and the total value of the stock you'll acquire, both remain unchanged.

Stock dividends. We discussed cash dividends earlier. If a company distributes shares of stock instead of cash, it is making a *stock dividend.* As a general rule, a stock dividend is just a different way for the company to accomplish the same thing as a stock split. For example, if the company distributes one share for every share you already own, you end up with twice as many shares, which is the same result as a two for one stock split. If you hold stock options when your company declares a stock dividend, your options should be adjusted as described in the previous paragraph.

Stock certificates

Stock certificates are documents that represent ownership of shares. Certificates can be lost or destroyed, and transactions involving certificates are slow and expensive, so it rarely makes sense to obtain a certificate. Instead, your ownership will simply appear on the records of the brokerage firm where your shares are held.

Brokerage accounts

Shares you acquire as compensation, or by exercising an option, are normally transferred to a brokerage account set up in your name. If you're new to the world of stock investing, you should be aware that setting up a brokerage account is a simple procedure much like setting up a bank account. The main difference is that the account can hold shares of stock or other investments in addition to cash.

You'll quickly learn the simple procedures for buying and selling shares or other investments and obtaining cash from the account after you've sold shares.

To facilitate compliance with various regulations, most companies either require or encourage employees to use a particular brokerage firm for shares acquired as compensation. You may wish to use the same firm for your other investments, but you may find that another firm suits your needs better. Consider whether you're comfortable with a low-cost broker that expects you to handle the account with little assistance, or would prefer the kind of guidance and hand-holding you get from a full-service broker where fees are often higher. There are many brokers to choose from, and no single one is right for everyone.

Limit orders and stop orders

It's useful to educate yourself about the different kinds of orders you can place with your broker. If you simply tell the broker to sell shares, the broker will execute the transaction immediately at the best available price. That's called a *market order*, because you get whatever price is available in the market.

Sometimes it's better to place a *limit order.* You might say, for example, that you want to sell your shares, but only if the price is at least $40 per share. If the market price stays below $40, your sale won't go through, but you protect yourself against making the sale at a price you find unacceptable.

In other situations you may want to place a *stop order*. This is an order to sell these shares as quickly as possible if the market price drops below a specified level. You can use a stop order to reduce your risk of a major disaster.

> **Example:** You decided to hold shares of stock after exercising a stock option. The stock is currently trading at $40, and you hope it will go up to $50. You're willing to take the risk that

the stock will lose some of its value, but you can't afford to sell it for less than $30. You place a stop order to sell if the stock price drops below $32, figuring the broker should be able to get at least $30 per share if the order is activated.

✈ Stock prices can drop rapidly, especially if bad news arrives when the stock market is closed. A stop order doesn't always protect you against getting stuck with a significantly lower price. On May 6, 2010 we had a spooky "flash crash" in which stock prices fell off a cliff and then recovered minutes later. Many investors with stop loss orders found they had sold shares at an unacceptably low price during this event.

Identifying shares

You may find yourself in a situation where you hold different batches of shares that are exactly the same except for their tax characteristics. For example, you may have paid a higher price for some shares, or held only some of your shares long enough to have a long-term capital gain. If you decide to make a sale, but you aren't selling all your shares at the same time, it can make a big difference which shares you sell.

Example: You exercised an incentive stock option earlier this year, and then bought some additional shares in the same company on the open market. If you sell part of your holdings, it's important to know which shares you sold, because a sale of the ISO shares would create a disqualifying disposition.

If it isn't clear which shares you're selling, you can *identify* the shares at the time of the sale. When shares are held by a broker, this is a two-step process:

- *At the time of the sale,* specify to the broker which shares you're selling, *and then*

- *Within a reasonable time thereafter,* receive a written confirmation of that specification from the broker. (The written confirmation may be delivered electronically.)

These days it's often possible to identify shares as you place a sell order online, receiving your written confirmation instantly. Older methods are still available, however. If permitted by your broker, you can specify the shares you're selling over the telephone (this part doesn't have to be in writing) and receive written confirmation later, possibly on a confirmation slip the broker sends you in the mail.

 Selling the wrong shares can be an expensive mistake, so check ahead of time to make sure there won't be any problem securing the desired result when you plan to identify shares for sale.

If you don't identify the shares at the time of the sale, the IRS treats you as if you sold the oldest shares first. When you *want* to sell the oldest shares first, you don't have to identify the shares you're selling. And of course you don't have to identify shares when you sell all your holdings of that stock at one time. You only have to identify shares when you want to sell newer shares while continuing to hold older shares.

Some people think it's okay to wait until you prepare your tax return to determine which shares you sold, but that's an urban legend. You have to identify shares at the time of the sale.

Restrictions on selling

If you acquire stock from your company, you're likely to face restrictions on selling that don't apply to most shareholders. Here's a quick rundown of what you might face.

- **Vesting.** Companies often impose a vesting requirement for stock or options provided as compensation. That means you have to wait a specified period of time before you have full ownership rights, and you can't sell the stock during that period.

- **Blackout periods.** For the protection of outside investors, companies usually prevent employees from selling shares immediately before or after the annual or quarterly reports come out, or at other sensitive times. The times when you aren't allowed to sell shares are called *blackout periods*, and the times when you *can* sell may be called *window periods*.

- **Rule 144 stock.** You may receive stock that is subject to *Rule 144*, a regulation under the securities laws. You'll have a waiting period before you can sell these shares, and you may have to deal with additional limitations even after the waiting period is over. Your company will provide details about this rule if it applies to you.

- **Rule 701 stock.** This is another regulation under the securities laws, somewhat similar to Rule 144 but with different requirements. Here again, the company will provide details if the rule applies to you.

- **Lockup period.** If you work for a privately held company that goes public, you may find that you aren't allowed to sell shares during a *lockup period* of six months or so after the public offering.

It's important to take these restrictions into account when planning a strategy for your stock or options. For example, you may adopt a strategy where it's important to be able to sell shares by the end of the year. If you're dealing with blackout periods, your deadline is the end of the last window period in the year, which may be weeks earlier than December 31. Bear in mind also that selling shares under Rule 144 through a broker may take more time than usual.

4

Understanding Stock Prices

Stock prices don't work the way most people think they work.

MANY OF THE MOST COSTLY MISTAKES I've seen in handling stock and options—and believe me, I've seen some doozies—involved a misunderstanding of stock prices. These mistakes weren't limited to beginners. Many were made by experienced investors, including people with formal training in finance. Some were made by high ranking executives. I urge you to read this chapter even if you believe you already understand how stock prices work.

If you're new to investing, or want to fill gaps in your general knowledge of the subject, you may enjoy my book *That Thing Rich People Do*.

Where stock prices come from

Stock prices are not actually set by anyone. A stock quotation you see in the newspaper or on your computer screen is simply the price at which the last reported sale took place (often with a 15 to 20 minute delay). The price was determined by the amount buyers were bidding and sellers were asking at the time. Prices change automatically based on the buy and sell orders of investors.

> A stock goes up if demand exceeds the number of shares people are willing to sell at the current price. When there aren't enough buyers at the current price to purchase the shares offered for sale, the stock goes down.

800-pound gorillas

Millions of investors participate in the stock market, but a much smaller number of *institutional investors* (mutual funds, insurance companies and so forth) dominate the scene. Any one of these institutions may have billions of dollars to invest; in the aggregate they have many *trillions*. They compete ferociously with one another. As a practical matter, stock prices are the result of trading activity by the stock market's 800-pound gorillas.

With so much money riding on the outcome, they hire the best investment managers they can. These professionals are talented and hard working, and draw on enormous resources for research and analysis. When they determine that a stock is priced low enough to be an excellent investment, they buy shares of that stock—and keep buying until the price pushes up to a level where the stock is no longer a great bargain. Similarly, when the facts indicate that a stock is priced too high, the pros sell shares, and keep selling until the price drops low enough to once again turn the stock into a reasonably good investment.

In the blink of an eye

The price adjustments caused by the activities of professional money managers usually occur very quickly. When new information becomes available indicating that a stock is more valuable (or less valuable) than it previously appeared, the investors who react fastest gain the greatest benefit, buying at the lowest price or selling at the highest price. The time required for the stock market to react to significant news about a stock is measured in *seconds*, not hours or days.

If it appears that the market is reacting slowly to a news story, that's because the facts (or the *importance* of the facts) can't be determined right away. It took months for Enron's stock price to collapse because at first no one knew just how much bad news would crawl out from under that rock. The stock market reacted quickly to the available news, but the news itself came out slowly over a period of time.

The future is now

When the pros figure out how much money to pay for shares of a particular stock, they pay some attention to where the company is now, but much more to where they expect the company to be in the future. If it appears likely that a company will do well, this expectation will be reflected in a higher stock price before the strong performance actually occurs. Similarly, if it appears that the company is in for a rough patch, professional investors won't wait for an official announcement of the bad news before knocking the price down to a level that reflects difficulties the company will face in the future. This is why the financial pages often carry stories like this one from the September 23, 2004 *Wall Street Journal*:

> FedEx Corp., lifted by strong gains in shipment volume across almost all its deliver businesses, reported that its fiscal first-quarter profit more than doubled and said it sees no signs of a letup heading into

the peak shipping season. Despite the upbeat message, FedEx shares skidded $3.48, or 3.9% . . .

A company reports terrific results, but the stock price goes *down*. Illogical? Not at all. The pros were expecting strong profits, so they bid up the stock price before the announcement. The stock went down because investors were hoping for *even more* good news.

It can work the other way, too. There's a huge jury verdict against a company requiring payment of hundreds of millions of dollars, and the stock price goes *up*. Investors were expecting a verdict at least this bad, so now that the company no longer faces this problem the stock is worth more.

> The company's expected performance is "built into" the stock price. The only future events that aren't reflected in the stock price are *unexpected* events.

Implications

This brief description of some of the key principles about stock prices is enough to let us draw some conclusions—and avoid the most common mistakes made by investors. The most important implications are what I call the *fair pricing principle* and the *future pricing principle*.

Fair pricing principle. For any given stock at any given time, the price is very likely to be at a level where institutional investors believe the stock is a good investment. You can pick any stock at random and expect this to be true. If there were some objective way to know the stock was a bad investment, the pros would sell enough shares to lower the price. Likewise, if there were an objective way to know the stock was an outstanding investment (not just a good one), the pros would buy enough shares to raise the price. All stocks at all times are priced within a narrow range where it is difficult to tell the best investments from the worst ones.

This is not to say the prices established by trading among these experts are always right. They are frequently wrong, and sometimes *spectacularly* wrong. The trouble is, there's no way for you to know in advance which stock prices are too high or too low. If you can figure it out, the pros can figure it out too, and adjust their buying and selling decisions accordingly.

One important conclusion is that you can be confident your company's stock is fairly priced. In other words, it is priced at a level where the world's most astute analysts, acting on the basis of all available information, believe the stock is likely to perform reasonably well. You don't have to spend time and energy figuring out that your company's stock is a good investment. Professional investors have done the work for you, calculating a reasonable price level for the stock and bidding it up or down to that level.

Future pricing principle. The current price for your company's stock takes expected future performance into account. That means the stock can be a good investment even if the company is going through hard times. Unfortunately, it also means your company's stock has a risk of losing value, even if the company is doing well, and will continue to do well in the future. Strong performance that can be predicted by professional investors is built into the stock price long before it actually occurs, and that means excellent results will not necessarily propel the stock to higher levels. The stock can do poorly even while the company does well.

This is one of the most important points to understand, and also one of the most difficult ones to accept. If your company is performing well, it may be hard to believe there's a risk that the stock price will fall. Keep in mind that a stock without any risk would be the best investment in the stock market. As soon as the pros figured out that there was little or no risk in your company's stock, they would buy as many shares as possible—until the price rose to a level where the stock had just as much risk of loss as any other stock.

At one time or another in the last several years, most of the elite "blue chip" stocks in the Dow Jones Industrial Average have lost more than half their value. Many strong, innovative, profitable technology companies have lost more than *80%* of their value. Stocks can be good investments, but they are never risk-free.

Avoiding common mistakes

There's a simple way to evaluate statements about the future price of your company's stock. Just ask yourself how professional investors would react if the statement were true, and what that would mean for the *current* stock price. In many cases, you'll realize that the statement can't be true unless the country's most capable stock analysts—the ones working for mutual funds and other huge investors—are asleep at the switch.

This stock is a lousy investment. Companies sometimes go through extended periods when the stock price doesn't go up. People can get discouraged and feel that the stock is likely to continue its poor performance. At that point you may be tempted to believe that the stock or options you receive from your company have little value. Yet that would mean the big institutional investors that have enough clout to affect the stock price are missing a chance to improve their performance. Keep in mind that even in tough times—*especially* in tough times—a lot of hard-nosed analysts are taking a careful look at your company's stock. If they can determine that it's overpriced, their selling activity will quickly bring the price down to a level where that's no longer true. And that means you can reasonably conclude that the stock is a good investment at the current price, even if it has done poorly in the recent past.

This stock is a safe investment. Many people feel that the stock of the company where they work is a safe investment. They may get that impression because things are going well for the company:

products are selling, profits are rising, morale is good. Or they may get that impression based on the way the stock has performed in the past: it's gone up steadily for the last five years, so surely it will continue to rise.

There are many reasons your company's stock can go down even while the company performs well. Investors may sell stocks because they expect a downturn in the overall economy, or because interest rates went up, making bonds look like a more attractive investment. Or they may simply have raised their expectations for your company so high that even a strong performance is disappointing.

Investors *love* safe investments. If your company's stock is truly safe, the pros of the investing world are missing a great opportunity to make an investment that has profit potential but no risk of loss. They should be buying shares at this "safe" level until the price rises to a level where this stock bears a risk of loss. This logic should tell you that professional money managers believe your company's stock is a risky investment—just like every other stock. There's no such thing as a stock investment that doesn't involve risk of loss.

The leading analyst in this industry set a target price 50% above the current price. Really? That means all the analysts working for the big institutional investors are pretty stupid, letting this amazing bargain sit there when they could juice their returns by snapping up shares at today's bargain price. When you see a statement like this, you can be certain that a majority of Wall Street's best analysts disagree.

The stock price recently fell by 50%, so it makes sense to hold on until the stock price recovers. This is an especially dangerous misconception for people who exercise stock options and then see the price fall while holding the shares. It's hard to admit that the smart thing to do might be to sell the shares now if you could have sold them at a much higher price earlier. Think about it: this stock has to double in price (go up 100%) to get back to its recent value.

Here again, professional investors are acting foolishly if they're ignoring a chance to buy shares that have a strong likelihood of doubling in a short period of time. You can be certain these pros believe a recovery of that magnitude is highly unlikely. The recent stock price doesn't tell you where the stock price is going in the future.

The bottom line

It would be wrong to suggest that all stocks are exactly equally good investments. There are plenty of people who make a living by analyzing stocks to figure out which ones will do better. The key point is that there are so many of these people, and they do their job so well, that stock prices adjust to levels that make it extremely difficult to tell in advance which ones will perform better than others.

You should never think of your company's stock as a bad investment. The stock market's bidding process assures you that the price is at a level where the best analysts believe the stock is a good investment. At the same time, you should never assume your company's stock is immune from losing value, even if you work for a great company. Up to a point, the risk of loss can be well worth taking, but you mustn't fool yourself into thinking the risk isn't there.

5

Understanding Investment Risk

If your stock or options become valuable enough, it will be important for you to understand investment risk.

IF YOU'RE LIKE MOST PEOPLE, you won't look at the stock or options you receive from your company exactly the same as other investments. For one thing, you didn't take money from your savings to buy these items, you *earned* them. In a real sense, they represent sweat equity. What's more, they provide you with a way to participate in the success of the company where you work. Continuing to hold them demonstrates your commitment to the company and faith in its future. You may not want to cash out merely because some other investment approach is theoretically a little better.

At some point, though, your equity compensation may grow in value to become a significant part of your net worth. When that happens, investment risk becomes an important factor in your financial life. That's a problem you want to have—but nevertheless a problem. Failure to deal with it properly can be a costly mistake.

Size matters

In April 2004, a 32-year-old British man named Ashley Revell sold everything he had—investments, home, auto, even most of his clothes—and flew to Las Vegas where he bet every last penny, more than $135,000, on a single spin of the roulette wheel. He was planning to bet on black, but changed his mind at the last minute and bet on red. He won!

Most would agree that Mr. Revell's gamble was unwise, even though it turned out well for him. Revell himself said afterward that it was a crazy thing to do. His father's comment: "He's a naughty boy."

We don't call someone crazy when they bet $2 at roulette, though. Viewed purely as a financial transaction, it's a poor "investment," because the average payoff is less than $2. What's more, there's a significant risk—more than 50%—of losing 100% of the amount wagered in a single bet. Yet the amount wagered is too small to produce a financial disaster. You may approve or disapprove of this form of entertainment, but small-stakes gambling, pursued in moderation, doesn't place the gambler's financial health at risk.

Gambling on stock options. The *Wall Street Journal* ran a story describing what happened to two women who performed consulting services for the same Internet company. Each was given a choice between cash compensation—a few thousand dollars—or stock options that might become valuable but could also turn out to be worthless. One took cash and the other took options.

In a situation like this, it's a lot harder to figure the odds of success than in a casino. Plenty of people who accepted stock or options as compensation have ended up with worthless paper. In this particular case, the woman who took the options became a millionaire (on paper, at least) when Google, the Internet company that gave her the options, went public.

Was she like Ashley Revell, someone who took a crazy risk and got lucky? Not really. Even if the options ended up being worthless, she wouldn't have been noticeably worse off than the woman who took cash. In the grand scheme of things she wouldn't have missed a few thousand dollars. In fact, the *Journal* reported that the woman who took the cash couldn't remember how she spent it. The risk involved in taking the options was a reasonable one, even though there was a real possibility of total loss, because the loss wouldn't have been that painful, and the potential reward was great.

Key principle. When you consider what to do with the stock or options you receive from your company, think about how much impact this is likely to have on your financial future. I've seen people gamble with millions of dollars' worth of stock or options, taking even more risk than Ashley Revell. Some got lucky, turning their millions into even more millions. Others lost everything, and even ended up with tax debts they couldn't pay.

When you're dealing with hundreds of dollars, or even a few thousand, go with your heart. Take some risk if that feels like the right thing to do. If the risk makes you uncomfortable, play your hand conservatively. The outcome won't change your lifestyle, so the best approach is one that fits your personality.

When you start dealing with amounts that can affect your financial future, you have a responsibility to yourself, and to anyone who relies on you for support, to think like an investor. That doesn't mean avoiding all risk. It simply means keeping your risk within reasonable limits.

Frame of reference

To gain some perspective on investment risk, let's consider what kind of portfolio a professional might recommend if you had a good chunk of money and complete freedom to invest any way you want. You might get many different opinions from different advisors, but those in the mainstream would probably say something like this:

- Figure out how much you should set aside for emergencies. Put this amount into a money market fund or the equivalent, where losses are highly unlikely and you can quickly convert it to cash. Don't overdo it, though, because the earnings from this type of account are so paltry they may not even keep pace with inflation.

- Divide the rest between stocks and bonds. Stocks produce higher returns, but at higher risk. Prior to retirement, most people should have at least half their portfolio in stocks, and it makes sense to push that percentage higher, perhaps to 80% or more, if you're young and you're comfortable with that much risk.

- The stock and bond portfolios should be diversified and unleveraged, as explained below.

A portfolio set up this way can be expected to provide a healthy rate of growth over the long run. There are many ways to tweak this general formula, but in broad outline this is essentially what most advisors would recommend for most people.

> The stock portion of the portfolio, no matter how well managed, will lose value from time to time, sometimes sharply. Yet it makes sense to hold stocks if you can weather those bad stretches because the average growth rate is faster for stocks than for other investments.

Here's the key point. Most advisors would recommend against taking significantly more investment risk than you have when you hold a diversified, unleveraged portfolio of 80% stocks and 20% bonds. If you go far beyond that risk level, you're heading into Ashley Revell territory. Yet people who receive stock or options from their company sometimes take twice that much risk, or four times as much, or more. The big issues here are leverage and concentration.

Leverage

If you make an investment with borrowed money, finance experts say you're using *leverage.* The effect is to multiply your profits if the investment goes up—and multiply your losses if it goes down.

> **Example:** You use $5,000 of your own money and $5,000 borrowed in a margin loan to buy $10,000 worth of stock in XYZ company. If the value of the stock declines 20%, the $2,000 loss represents *40%* of your $5,000 equity in this stock.

Investing on margin is highly profitable for the brokers who make the margin loans, but rarely a good idea for investors. The potential for increased profits can make margin investing seem attractive, but you also have a potential for increased losses. Leverage is a risk multiplier, and the added risk you take is not the "good" kind of risk that enhances your prospects for long-term success.

Hidden leverage. If you borrow money to make an investment, you're aware of the debt and should be aware of the added risk. Sometimes leverage is less obvious. This is particularly true when you're going to have a large tax bill next April. Strictly speaking, you don't have a debt obligation until April 15, but once the tax obligation is locked in, it has the same effect on your level of risk.

> **Example:** It's January, and you hold $1,000,000 worth of stock. On April 15 you'll have to come up with $400,000 in federal and state taxes. A realistic assessment of your wealth at this point would place it at $600,000. If the stock value goes down 20% during the next three months, you'll lose

one-third of your equity. In other words, you're in the same position as if you borrowed $400,000 to make this investment.

This can be a dangerous form of leverage. If the stock goes down more than 60%, the proceeds from a sale of the stock won't be enough to cover your taxes. You're probably thinking you don't have to worry about such an unlikely event. Recent history teaches us otherwise.

> Be extremely cautious when dealing with a situation where you have a large unpaid tax liability looming in the future.

Diversification

Avoiding leverage doesn't get you home free. If your investments aren't diversified, you can be exposed to risk that's twice as high, or even four times as high, as if you hold a diversified portfolio. We saw earlier that a portfolio that's weighted heavily toward stocks can be near the high end of the spectrum for reasonable investment risk. If you take two to four times that much risk, you are off the scale. You may get lucky, like Ashley Revell did, but you aren't being smart.

Your portfolio is *diversified* when it is divided among a large number of stocks, without heavy concentration in any one company, or in any one industry or segment of the economy. Your investments are not diversified if half your wealth is tied up in the stock of a single company. Ditto if you divide your wealth among 100 companies, but they're all tech stocks (or pharmaceutical stocks, or whatever other flavor appeals to you). Broad diversification is the single most important principle of sound investing.

One reason is that diversification is such a powerful force in reducing risk. The amount of risk in a diversified portfolio can be measured statistically, and it's often a small fraction of the risk you take by holding a single stock. Here's a chart that illustrates the point.

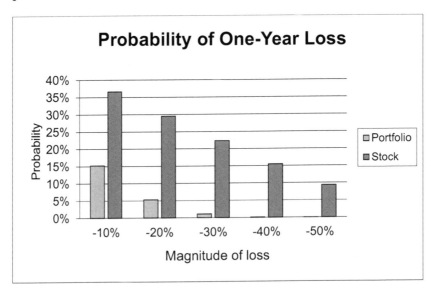

This chart compares the risk of loss over a period of one year for a diversified portfolio with the risk of loss for a single stock (20% volatility vs. 60% volatility). Both are assumed to grow at an average rate of 10%, but the average includes some losing years as well as winning years. For the diversified portfolio, it isn't unusual to see a 10% loss in the course of a year, and you can't rule out the possibility of a loss as large as 30%. Yet the probabilities of those losses are much smaller than for a single stock. You would almost never see a well-diversified portfolio decline in value by 40% or more in one year, but for a single stock with this much volatility it happens roughly one year out of six.

> The Nasdaq Index, which is *not* well diversified, declined nearly 40% in the year 2000, while the broader stock market declined only about 10%.

There's another important point. The added risk you take when you fail to diversify—professionals call it *concentration risk*—increases your risk of loss without enhancing your prospects for long-term success. When you shift your investments from bonds to stocks, you take more risk, but you're compensated for that risk. That's because in the long run, stocks tend to provide better returns than bonds. When you fail to diversify, you're taking more risk without getting an investment that's likely to provide better returns. That means concentration risk is *uncompensated* risk, like the kind you take if you bet on a roulette wheel.

Concentration risk should be measured based on your total wealth, not just the part that's in a particular account. You can reduce the risk you bear from your stock options by making diversified investments in your 401k account, for example. On the other hand, if your 401k account is invested in your company's stock, it increases your exposure to uncompensated risk.

Your company's stock and options

By definition, the equity compensation you receive from your company depends on the performance of a single stock. That isn't a problem if you have other investments that are well diversified, and your equity compensation is a small fraction of your net worth. You can think of the stock and options you receive from your company as part of your overall diversified portfolio, even if they aren't in the same investment account.

The issue becomes important when the value of your holdings in stock or options of your company becomes a large percentage of your wealth. As I said earlier, it's a good problem to have, because it means your equity compensation has made a big contribution to your wealth. Yet it's an important to deal with this risk before it deals with you.

Misconceptions. There are three common misconceptions that prevent many people from dealing effectively with the risk they face when holding a great deal of their company's stock. One is a belief that their own company's stock is safer than others, and even safer than a diversified portfolio of stocks. It's probably natural to feel that way when you work for an excellent company, so you have to remind yourself that the company and the stock are two different things. Stock experts can measure risk using statistical techniques, and there is no doubt at all that your company's stock exposes you to more risk—probably *a lot* more risk—than a diversified portfolio. It's like betting everything on one spin of the roulette wheel instead of dividing your money into hundreds or thousands of smaller bets.

A second misconception is the idea that you can control risk by acting in accordance with a careful, professional analysis of the stock. Analysis of that kind may help you build a good portfolio, but it doesn't allow you to make reliable predictions about any one stock. That's true no matter who did the analysis. The price of a stock can fall when all the analysts are positive, and even bubbling with enthusiasm. A good stock manager is like a good baseball manager. He can pick a lineup that has a good chance of winning, but has no way to predict whether a particular player will hit a home run, strike out or hit into a double play.

> The only reliable prediction about the stock market is one that was made many years ago by financier J.P. Morgan. Asked what the stock market was going to do, he replied, "It will fluctuate."

Another approach that makes sense to a lot of people is to "keep an eye on" the stock. They figure they can't lose much if they watch the stock price on a regular basis and head for the exits when things start to look bad. Sounds reasonable, but it doesn't work. Stock prices zigzag up and down all the time. When the price falls a little, you can't tell if that's the start of a larger drop or just a little jiggle you shouldn't worry about. When it falls a bit more, it could be the start of a downward trend or a "dip" that will attract bargain hunters to bid the price back up again. Looking at a chart of past performance, it's easy to see an overall pattern, but at the time it's happening you can't tell whether the next move will be up or down.

Thousands of employees at Enron kept their eye on the stock throughout a lengthy collapse, thinking at each step of the way that the worst must be over, until their shares became completely worthless.

Diversifying. If your holdings expose you to too much risk from your company's stock, the most obvious approach is to cash in some of those shares and invest the proceeds in a way that reduces your risk. Mutual funds provide a convenient way to diversify into a large number of stocks. Just make sure you are diversifying broadly, not buying a mutual fund that specializes in a narrow segment of the economy. You can reduce risk even further by putting some of the money into bonds, real estate or other non-stock investments.

You don't have to sell all your shares to achieve diversification. Your goal is to sell enough so the remaining shares don't expose you to an inappropriate level of risk. The number of shares you should continue to hold depends on many factors, including your overall financial condition, tax situation, age, family responsibilities, goals, risk tolerance and the strength of your desire (if any) to remain invested in your company's stock. Because these factors can vary widely, there is no rule of thumb that applies to all people. Nevertheless, if you're looking for a number that makes sense for most people, I would suggest holding no more than 20% of your wealth in your company's stock except in unusual circumstances, and preferably less than 10%. That's considerably more than the level that produces ideal diversification, but keeps your holdings within a range where the worst case scenario isn't likely to have a devastating effect on your finances.

Worth noting. Some advisors point out that your employer's stock exposes you to a double risk. If things go poorly at your company, the stock price could decline at the same time the company is cutting salaries or laying off workers. Keep this in mind as you decide how much risk to take with your company's stock.

If you can't (or won't) sell

The remainder of this book includes a great deal of information about the tax consequences and other considerations in exercising stock options and selling shares. What if you *can't* cash in now, or you have a strong reason not to do so? How can you manage risk in that situation?

If you're exposed to a lot of risk from your company's stock or options, it's a good idea to keep your other investments as "quiet" as possible. Minimize your exposure to this stock in your 401k or other accounts. Avoid high-risk approaches like margin investing. If you love tech stocks, get over it. Diversify your other stock investments as broadly as possible, or better still, move a larger than usual percentage of your other investments into more conservative investments, such as money market funds or bonds (avoiding long-term bonds and junk bonds). If one half of your house is exposed to a storm, make the other half as safe and cozy as you can.

In some situations you can gain protection against painful losses by placing a *stop order* with your stock broker, as described in Chapter 3. For example, if the stock is trading at $40 and you feel you can risk losing 20% of that value (to $32), you might place a stop order to sell if the stock price drops below $35. In most cases the broker will be able to execute this order at or above $32.

A stop order can be useful, but it has some limitations. You can't place a stop order until you own the shares and have the right to sell them, so you can't use this technique if your wealth is tied up in stock options or in shares that aren't vested. Once you get over that hurdle, you still may have to deal with blackout periods when you can't sell the shares. Those are precisely the periods when the stock price is most likely to move sharply, because they occur before and after the public release of your company's financial results and other important information. Finally, you should be aware that the stock price could drop quickly through the stop loss price you establish, as happened to many people during the "flash crash" in May 2010. An order to sell when the price drops below $35 doesn't provide complete assurance that the sale will occur at a price close to that number.

Chapter 32 discusses some other ways to protect gains without selling shares.

6

Income Tax Background

Here are the key principles you need to have in mind about federal income tax as you read the rest of this book.

THERE ARE A LOT OF TRICKY TAX RULES for stock options and other forms of equity compensation. We'll discuss them throughout the book, and explain how to use them to your best advantage. This chapter provides background information on some of the more general principles.

Two basic flavors

All of the income and deductions you may have are divided into two categories: *ordinary* income and loss, and *capital* gain and loss. Ordinary income includes your wages, of course, and also includes many other types of income: interest, dividends, pension and IRA income, alimony income—the list goes on, because it includes everything *other than* capital gain.

So what is capital gain? You have capital gain or loss when you sell a *capital asset,* which includes stock and anything else of lasting value. As a general rule, the income you report when you *receive* stock is considered compensation income, which means it is ordinary income, not capital gain. Yet when you sell those shares, any additional profit or loss is capital gain or loss.

As a result, equity compensation can result in ordinary income, capital gain, or some of both. In some cases, the amount of income you have from ordinary income rather than capital gain depends on when you exercise an option, or how long you hold your stock, or even whether you make a special filing with the IRS called a *section 83b election.*

> Qualifying dividends are something of a hybrid: under current law they're taxed at the same rates as long-term capital gain even though they're treated as ordinary income for other purposes.

Tax rates

The tax law has one set of rates for wages and other forms of ordinary income, and a different set of rates for long-term capital gain and qualifying dividends. The current (2014) rates for ordinary income took effect in 2013: 10%, 15%, 25%, 28%, 33%, 35%, and 39.6%. These rates apply in a series of steps. The first chunk of income is taxed at 10%, then the next is taxed at 15%, and so on. The total amount of tax you pay is actually a blend of these rates. You might end up paying income tax equal to 17% of your income, for example, where part of your income is taxed at 10%, another part is taxed at 15%, and the rest is taxed at 25%.

The rates for long-term capital gain are 0%, 15% and 20%. The 0% rate for long-term capital gain applies only while all your taxable income (including the capital gain, but after claiming deductions) is less than the amount that gets you into the 25% tax bracket. The 20%

rate for capital gain kicks in at the level where the 39.6% rate begins to apply to ordinary income.

> As you can see, it's a big advantage to have long-term capital gain instead of ordinary income.

Withholding. Withholding rates are designed to be approximately equal to the blended rate you'll end up paying, so the amount withheld from your paycheck doesn't necessarily match any of the rates listed above. Most companies use a special flat rate (now set at 25%) when they have to withhold on special income items, such as when you exercise a stock option. Bear in mind that your actual tax rate on that income can be as high as 39.6%, so you can end up owing quite a bit more tax than the amount that was withheld.

Tax brackets. If your income falls in the range where the last chunk is taxed at 28%, we say you're in the 28% *tax bracket*. That information can be useful in estimating how much additional tax you'll pay if you have added income—for example, from exercising a stock option. Keep in mind, though, that added income can push you up into the next tax bracket. You don't get to stay in the 28% tax bracket just because that's where you are when you count your regular wage income.

Stock as income

We tend to think of income as the amount of cash received, but you may have to report income (and pay income tax) when you receive shares of stock—even before you've had a chance to sell those shares. We'll cover these rules in detail, including exceptions that may apply. For now, the main point is that it's incorrect to equate income with cash. The tax law says, with some exceptions, that income includes the value of any stock you receive from your employer.

When you think about it, you'll realize that's not at all surprising. If people only had to pay tax on their cash income, wealthy executives would take nearly all their compensation in the form of stock and pay little or no income tax. Ordinary employees who need cash to pay their bills would pay more tax than the big shots.

Yet this rule creates your most important potential tax problem in dealing with equity compensation. You can have a tax obligation—which must be paid in cash—at a time when you haven't received any cash you can use to pay that tax. What's more, the tax obligation doesn't necessarily go away, or even become smaller, if the value of your stock declines. It's important to think of the stock itself as income, and plan carefully for the corresponding tax obligation.

Compensation income

We're frequently going to say that a particular event causes you to have *compensation* income. This is ordinary income, taxed at rates up to 39.6%. If you're an employee, it will be reported on Form W-2. In the following cases it's subject to income tax withholding and social security tax:

- You receive a grant of vested stock (or make the section 83b election for unvested stock).
- Your previously unvested stock vests (assuming you didn't make the section 83b election).
- You exercise a nonqualified stock option.

There's a special rule for income from selling shares acquired through employee stock purchase plans or incentive stock options. As explained later, some or all of that income may be treated as compensation income. You should see it appear on Form W-2 as part of your wages, but this income is *not* subject to withholding or social security tax. If you examine your W-2 closely, you may find the figure for your "social security wages" is smaller than the figure for total wages.

> Whenever you have income that isn't subject to withholding, you have to be especially careful to plan for the tax you'll have to pay.

Meeting the withholding requirement. Even if your income arrives in the form of shares of stock, the IRS expects to receive withholding and social security payments in cash. Your employer has the obligation to collect this money and pay it to the IRS, but *you* have the obligation to pay it. Sometimes the company helps out by providing some form of cash compensation, but in most cases you have to come up with this money. Often that means selling some of the shares to cover the withholding, although you're allowed to pay this amount without selling shares if you can raise the cash from other resources.

Components of withholding. Federal income tax withholding is designed to cover some or all of your income tax liability for the compensation income. If your state has an income tax, you can expect state income tax withholding as well. You'll also have to pay social security tax. This tax currently applies at the rate of 7.65% on compensation income up to $117,000 (for 2014) and 1.45% on compensation income above that level. Since 2013, high-income taxpayers have had to pay an additional 0.9% hospital insurance tax on compensation above specified levels.

Non-employees. If you receive compensation income without being an employee, there won't be any withholding. You'll owe income tax and self-employment tax, and you may be required to make quarterly payments of estimated tax.

Calculating capital gain or loss

Even if you report compensation income upon receiving stock, you'll report capital gain or loss when you sell the shares. Normally, this is the difference between the amount you received from the sale and the amount you paid for the shares. Certain adjustments are required to make sure you don't pay double tax on the same income. To use more precise terminology, you'll calculate the difference between the *amount realized* on the sale and your *adjusted basis* for the shares.

Amount realized. The amount realized when you sell shares of stock is what you received for the sale, including any debts that were paid from the sale proceeds. If you sell stock through a broker, the amount realized is the selling price of the stock minus the brokerage commission and any other expenses of sale.

Adjusted basis. Adjusted basis is a way to measure your investment in an asset, but with some special rules. The most important one for our purposes says that if you report income from receiving an asset, you get to include that income as part of your adjusted basis. For example, if your employer grants stock to you worth $5,000, you'll report $5,000 of income—and you'll own the stock with a basis of $5,000. If you sell it for $5,600, you'll report a gain of $600, even though you never actually paid for the stock. It's as if your employer paid you $5,000 in cash and you used the money to buy the stock.

Basis can be adjusted in other ways, too. For example, suppose you bought 100 shares of stock at $30, paying a $40 brokerage commission. Your basis is $3,040, or $30.40 per share. Then the stock splits two for one, so you have 200 shares where you had 100 before. You didn't pay any additional money to acquire these shares, so your investment didn't increase. Your total basis is still $3,040, but now it's divided among all the shares. When you sell the stock, you'll report the sale as if you paid $15.20 per share.

Withholding tax paid when you received your shares is not included in your basis for the shares.

Form 1099-B. Early in the year, usually near the end of January or early in February, brokers send *Form 1099-B* to customers who sold stocks or other securities during the preceding year. For stock sales, these forms report the number of shares sold and the proceeds of the sale (the amount of money received). Beginning with the 2011 tax year, these forms also include the basis (used to calculate gain or loss) and holding period (short-term or long term) of the shares sold in some transactions.

For many investors, the added information about basis and holding period can be helpful in preparing their tax returns. You should be aware, however, that for some transactions Form 1099-B will continue to show how much you received for a sale of shares without reporting your basis for the shares. That doesn't mean you have zero basis; it means you'll have to use your own records (and the rules explained in this book) to determine the basis of those shares.

What's more, the basis shown on the form won't always be correct, even if your broker follows all the rules. In particular, when you exercise an option, the correct basis of your shares includes the purchase price plus any compensation income you report as a result of exercising the option, but the broker may report only the purchase price as your basis. You'll have to make the adjustment for compensation income when you prepare your return. Otherwise you'll end up paying double tax on that income. See Chapter 30 for more details.

Tax treatment of capital gains

We noted earlier the huge tax advantage for income that qualifies as long-term capital gain. If you have a long-term capital gain that isn't wiped out by a capital loss, your tax rate on that gain can be 20 percentage points lower than for ordinary income. To qualify for the lower rate, you have to hold the asset at least until the anniversary of *the day after* the day you acquired it. For example, if you buy shares on June 7, you have to sell on or after June 8 of the following year to have a long-term capital gain.

Your holding period may not begin until the vesting date, as explained later.

You may also have *short-term* capital gains. These are gains from selling an asset you held one year or less. Short-term capital gain is taxed at the same rates as ordinary income. No special tax break there. But short-term capital gain can still be better than ordinary income. That's because of the way the tax law treats capital *losses*, as explained below.

Notice that if you sell stock on the anniversary of the date you acquired it, your gain or loss is short-term. You need to hold one more day to get long-term gain or loss.

Tax treatment of capital losses

Special rules apply to capital losses. Some capital losses aren't allowed as a deduction, and even when they *are* allowed, special limitations apply.

Capital losses not allowed. There are two main situations where you can't claim a loss from selling stock. One is a sale to a related person. For tax purposes, a trust or a business that's owned by you or your family can be considered a related "person." If you want to claim a deduction for a capital loss, you have to sell your shares to an unrelated person.

The other rule you need to know is called the *wash sale rule.* It says you can't claim a loss from selling stock if you buy shares of the same stock within 30 days before or after the sale that produced the loss.

> **Example:** You own 100 shares that cost you $25 per share, and the stock is now trading at $15. You'd like to deduct the loss, so you sell the shares. Yet you want to continue owning the shares, so you buy another 100 shares of the same stock a few days later at $16.

You have a loss of $1,000 on the sale, but you aren't allowed to deduct it. Instead, you add $1,000 to your basis for the replacement shares, so a sale of those shares will be reported as if you paid $26 per share instead of $16 per share. You would get the same result if you bought replacement shares a few days *before* you sold shares at a loss, because the *wash sale period* extends 30 days before and after the day you sell shares at a loss.

This rule applies only to losses. You can't eliminate a gain by purchasing replacement shares. For more on the wash sale rule, visit Fairmark.com.

Capital losses allowed. Just like capital gains, you have to divide capital losses between long-term and short-term. Then you apply them in the following order:

- First, deduct the loss against capital gains in the same category (long-term loss against long-term gain, short-term loss against short-term gain).

- Next, if you have overall loss in one category, deduct the loss against any gain that's left in the other category (long-term loss against short-term gain, or short-term loss against long-term gain).

- If you still have some capital loss left after these two steps, apply the loss against your ordinary income—but only up to $3,000 of capital loss ($1,500 if married filing separately).

- Any remaining amount of capital loss *carries over* to the next year, when you can use it just as if it were a brand-new loss for that year. If you still don't use all of it, you carry it to the next year, and so on.

Generally speaking, an *ordinary* deduction or loss is better than a capital loss. If you have an ordinary loss of $5,000, you don't have to worry about a $3,000 limit, and the loss will reduce your ordinary income. A *capital* loss will reduce your capital gain—the part of your income that may be taxed at a lower rate. Worse, if your capital loss is large enough, you may have to carry part of it to the next year, rather than using all of it to reduce taxes right away.

Part II
Restricted Stock

7

Terminology for Restricted Stock

People who receive restricted stock awards or restricted stock units need to add these terms to their vocabulary.

SOME COMPANIES MAKE IT POSSIBLE to receive shares of stock without paying for them. This chapter describes terminology used for two similar forms of benefit: restricted stock units and restricted stock awards.

Restricted stock units

A *restricted stock unit* is a right to receive stock after you've satisfied any conditions imposed by the company. By far the most common condition is simply continuing to work for the company for a period of time. If you still work there at the end of the specified period you receive the stated number of shares. You receive nothing, though, if your employment terminates before that date.

Other types of conditions are possible. You may receive shares only if you reach a sales goal or your department completes a project before a deadline. One way or another, a restricted stock unit requires you to earn the shares.

With this form of benefit you don't own shares until you've earned them in the way specified by the company. That means you won't receive dividends the company might pay prior to that date. Some companies provide a payment equivalent to the dividend, however. The terms of the restricted stock unit may provide that you receive this payment only if you succeed in earning the shares.

Restricted stock awards

A *restricted stock award*, sometimes called a *restricted stock grant* (or simply a *stock grant*), provides essentially the same benefit as a restricted stock unit. The difference is that shares are transferred to you at the time of the award, subject to a provision that you will forfeit the shares (in other words, the company will take them back) if you don't satisfy a condition. Here again, the most common condition is a requirement to continue working for the company for a stated period of time, but other conditions are possible.

In most cases the shares are held in escrow until you've satisfied the condition for earning the shares. This means someone else has possession of the shares even though you are the owner. An escrow arrangement makes it easier for the company to recover the shares if you forfeit them.

Although you don't have possession of the shares, the transfer into escrow makes you the owner. As the owner you may receive dividends and have an opportunity to participate in shareholder votes.

> The difference between a restricted stock unit and a restricted stock award can be insignificant. In one case you have to earn the right to receive shares, and in the other case your receive shares up front but have to earn the right to keep them.

Vesting terminology

Some special terminology is used when you receive shares with a possibility of forfeiting them later.

Vested. Shares are considered *vested* when you have earned the right to keep them. Prior to that date they are not vested. The time required for shares to become vested is sometimes called the *vesting period.*

> If you receive a restricted stock unit, you must satisfy the condition for earning the shares before they are transferred to you, so the shares are fully vested at the time you receive them. The concept of vesting after the transfer applies to restricted stock awards, not restricted stock units.

Substantial risk of forfeiture. During the vesting period there is a possibility you will fail to satisfy the vesting condition and have to return the shares to the company. This possibility means the stock is *subject to a substantial risk of forfeiture.* That's quite a mouthful, and simply means the stock isn't vested. I mention this term only because you may see it elsewhere and wonder where it fits in.

Section 83b election. When you receive stock that isn't vested, you can actually choose which of two sets of tax rules will apply to you. One set of tax rules applies if you do nothing, and a different set of rules applies if you file a *section 83b election.* This is a statement you file with the IRS within 30 days after you receive the stock saying that you want the alternate set of tax rules to apply. (For this purpose you "receive" the shares when they go into escrow, if your company uses an escrow arrangement.) You'll learn about the effects of this election in Chapters 8 and 9, and you can find more details concerning vesting and the section 83b election in Part VII.

8

Tax Rules for Restricted Stock

This chapter covers basic tax rules for restricted stock units and restricted stock awards. It also covers tax rules for a purchase of stock from your company, where the purchase isn't part of a stock option plan or employee stock purchase plan.

IT'S A GOOD IDEA TO READ THIS CHAPTER even if you're mainly interested in stock options or your company's ESPP. The tax rules in this chapter lay the foundation for the rules that apply to those other kinds of compensation. For now, though, we're concerned only with transactions where your company gives you a restricted stock unit or restricted stock award, or where you buy shares from your company *other than* a purchase that involves a stock option or ESPP. The rules discussed here cover purchases at full price as well as purchases at a discount.

> **Tax trap alert.** You may not think you need to worry about the tax consequences if you pay full value for stock you receive from your company. If the stock isn't vested at the time of purchase, though, your failure to make a section 83b election, as explained later, could be costly.

Three sets of rules. There are different rules for each of the following three situations:

- Your stock is *vested* when you receive it.

- Your stock is *not vested* when you receive it.

- Your stock is *not vested* when you receive it, and you file the *section 83b election.*

Generally your stock is *vested* if you can keep it (or sell it for full value) when your employment terminates. See Part VII for details on vesting and making the section 83b election.

Stock is vested

When you receive vested stock, you have to report compensation income for the year you receive it. The amount of income is the fair market value of the stock at the time you received it, reduced by the amount you paid for it, if any.

Restricted stock units. If you receive restricted stock units, this rule applies in the year you satisfy the vesting requirement and receive the shares, *not* in the year the RSU is granted. You will report income equal to the value of the shares on the vesting date. The value on the date the company originally granted the restricted stock unit doesn't affect your taxes in any way.

> **Example:** You receive a restricted stock unit at a time when the shares are worth $18,000, but the shares are worth $20,000 when you satisfy the vesting condition. You have to

report $20,000 of compensation income as of the vesting date in addition to all your other income for that year.

Paying for shares. If you pay something for the shares, other than tax withholding, the amount of compensation income is reduced by the amount you paid.

> **Example:** You buy $20,000 worth of stock from your company for $15,000. The stock is vested when you receive it. You have to report $5,000 of compensation income in addition to all your other income for that year.

As a reminder, we're talking here about a purchase where you are *not* using a stock option or participating in an employee stock purchase plan. Rules for those situations are discussed later.

Cashless income. Some people tend to associate *income* with *cash*. That isn't the case here. You have to report income, and pay tax, *even if you haven't sold the stock*. You didn't receive any cash—in fact, you may have paid cash to receive the stock—yet you have to come up with money to pay the IRS. Careful planning is essential!

The amount of tax you'll pay depends on your tax bracket. If the entire amount falls in the 28% bracket in the second example above, you'll pay 28% of $5,000, or $1,400 (plus any social security tax, self-employment tax or state income tax). If your bargain element is large, it's likely that some of the income will push up into a higher tax bracket than your usual one.

No capital gain. You may have capital gain later when you sell the stock. But the income you report now, when you *receive* the stock, is compensation income, not capital gain. Don't be confused by the fact that your compensation is in the form of stock.

Withholding. If you're an employee, the company is required to withhold on this compensation income. Of course the IRS insists on receiving withholding payments in cash, not in shares of stock. There are various ways the company can handle the withholding requirement. The most common one is simply to require you to pay the withholding amount in cash at the time you receive the stock.

Example: You have to report $25,000 of compensation income as a result of receiving vested shares. The company may require you to pay $9,000 to cover state and federal withholding requirements.

The amount paid must cover federal and state income tax withholding, and the employee share of social security tax and hospital insurance tax as well. The portion that is income tax withholding will be a credit against the tax you owe when you file your return at the end of the year. Be prepared: the amount of withholding won't necessarily be large enough to cover the full amount of the tax due on this income. You may end up owing tax on April 15 even if you paid withholding at the time you exercised the option, because the withholding amount is merely an estimate of the actual tax liability.

Example: You receive a stock grant valued at $10,000 and pay $2,500 in federal withholding. Depending on your tax bracket and other factors, the actual tax on this $10,000 of income may be $3,500 or more, which means you could end up owing more (or getting a smaller refund) on April 15.

Withholding and employment tax you pay when you receive your stock is *not* part of the purchase price. Don't include withholding in your basis when you sell the stock.

Some companies make it possible to sell some of the shares at the time of the transfer so you don't have to come up with cash out of pocket to pay the withholding.

Non-employees. If you're not an employee, withholding won't apply when you receive the stock. The income should be reported to you on Form 1099-MISC instead of Form W-2. Remember that this is compensation for services. In general this income will be subject to self-employment tax as well as federal and state income tax.

Tax consequences when you sell the stock. When you sell the stock, you're treated the same as if you had bought it on the date the company gave it to you, for an amount equal to the amount you paid (if any) *plus the amount of income you reported.* Even if you didn't actually pay anything for the stock, you have *basis* equal to the amount of income you reported. It's as if the company paid you that much cash and then you used the cash to buy the stock. If you sell the stock after holding it for a year or less, you'll have a short-term capital gain or loss on the sale. If you hold it for more than a year, your gain or loss will be long-term. It's important to keep a record of when you received the stock, the amount (if any) you paid for it and the amount of income you reported at that time.

> **Example:** You buy 1,000 shares of stock at $20 per share when the value is $50 per share. The stock is vested when you receive it, and you report $30,000 of compensation income. Fifteen months later you sell the stock for $60,000. Your basis includes the $20,000 you paid plus the $30,000 you reported as compensation income. The sale produces a $10,000 long-term capital gain.

Stock is not vested

If the stock isn't vested when you receive it, you have a choice of two different tax treatments. First we'll look at what happens under the general rule. Then we'll see what happens if you file a *section 83b election.*

Under the general rule, receiving stock that isn't vested is a pretty simple event. You report nothing at all at that time. You may *feel* richer if you didn't pay for the stock, or you bought it at a bargain price, but the tax law says you aren't richer until the stock vests. It isn't regular income, or AMT income, or even tax-exempt income. It's nothing at all. Your only obligation at this point is to maintain a record of what stock you acquired, when you received it and the amount (if any) you paid, so you can report the proper consequences later.

Dividends before vesting. If you receive stock (instead of restricted stock units), you own the stock while you're waiting for it to vest, so you may receive dividends during this period. Yet the tax law treats you as if you don't own the stock yet, so the company won't report these payments as dividends. Any dividends you receive during this period are treated as *compensation*. The company will report them on your W-2, *not* on Form 1099-DIV. That means they won't qualify for the 15% rate that applies to most dividend income. You get the benefit of that special tax rate only for dividends paid after the stock vests.

Tax consequences at vesting. If all goes well, you'll stay with the company long enough to own the stock outright. At that point— when the stock vests—you'll report compensation income equal to the difference between the fair market value of the stock and the amount (if any) you paid for it. In this case, *fair market value is determined on the vesting date*. If the value of the stock goes up while you're waiting for the stock to vest, you'll end up reporting that added value as compensation income, not capital gain, when the stock vests.

> **Example:** Your company lets you buy $10,000 worth of stock for $8,000. If your employment terminates within the following two years, you have to sell the stock back to the company for $8,000, the amount you paid. That means your stock isn't vested. You don't file the section 83b election, so you have no income to report in the year of purchase.
>
> Two years later you're still working for the company and the stock vests. At that time the stock is worth $15,000. You report $7,000 of compensation income: the current value of $15,000 minus your cost of $8,000.

The *Alves* trap. You can have a restriction that prevents your stock from being vested even if you pay full value for the stock. Because of a tax case called *Alves*, you may end up paying unnecessary tax in this situation. If the stock goes up in value before it vests, you'll have to report the increase as compensation income at that time. You can avoid this result by filing the section 83b election as explained below.

Tax consequences at sale. A sale of the stock after it's vested will result in capital gain or loss. Your basis will be the amount you paid for the stock plus the amount of income you reported at the time the stock became vested. Your gain or loss will be long-term if you held the stock more than a year after the *vesting date*. Otherwise any gain or loss will be short-term.

> **Example:** Let's continue with the previous example. Six months after the stock vests, you sell it for $20,000. You paid only $8,000 for the stock, but you reported $7,000 of income when the stock vested, so your basis for the stock is $15,000. You report only $5,000 of gain on the sale. Your gain is short-term, even though you held the stock 2½ years, because for tax purposes you're treated as if you acquired the stock on the date it vested.

Tax consequences of forfeiture. It's possible that you'll stop working for the company before the stock vests, and forfeit the stock or have to sell it back for the amount you paid for it—or less. If you sell it back for the same amount you paid to receive the stock, you report no gain or loss. You may feel that you've lost something, because the stock was worth more than you received in the forced sale. But you never included anything in income for that added value, so you can't reduce your income for the loss you suffered. You get no deduction in this situation.

> **Example:** We'll use the previous example one more time. You bought stock worth $10,000 for $8,000, but you reported

no income at the time because the stock wasn't vested. Before the stock vested, you left to work for another company and had to sell the stock back for the same $8,000 you originally paid, even though the stock was worth much more. You should report the sale on your tax return, but you have no gain or loss, so it doesn't affect the amount of tax you pay.

If you sell the stock back for *less than* $8,000, you'll report a capital loss.

Section 83b election

If you receive stock (not restricted stock units), you can change the consequences described above by filing a *section 83b election.* You send a notice to the IRS that includes certain information and declares that you want this election to apply. *This election must be filed within 30 days after you receive the stock.* (You're treated as receiving the stock when the company transfers it into escrow, even though you don't have physical possession of the shares at that time.) See Chapter 24 for details on making this election.

If you make the section 83b election, you're treated as if the shares were vested when you received them:

- You report compensation income at the time you receive the stock, measured by the value of the stock at that time. When you determine the value of the stock for this purpose, you have to ignore the existence of any temporary restriction. If the amount you pay is equal to the fair market value of the stock, the amount of income you report is zero.

- Dividends you receive before the stock vests will *not* be treated as compensation income. That means the dividends can qualify for the special 15% tax rate.

- You have nothing to report at the time the stock vests.

- When you sell the stock, your basis is the amount (if any) you paid for the stock plus the amount of income you reported when you received it. Your holding period goes back to that date, too, so any gain or loss will be long-term if more than a year has elapsed from the day you received the stock.

By far the most frequent problem with the section 83b election is missing the 30-day deadline. You can't wait until you file your tax return to make this election. You have to do it right away.

Tax consequences of forfeiture. It might seem logical to get a deduction if you forfeit stock after making the section 83b election. After all, you voluntarily reported income and paid tax as a result of making this election. A corresponding deduction when you forfeit the stock would make sense. Unfortunately, the law says you can't claim a deduction in this situation. Possibly this rule is designed to prevent people from using the section 83b election to manipulate their income in an artificial way. Whatever the reason, the law is clear: no deduction for a forfeiture.

Before making the section 83b election, be sure you consider the risk that you may forfeit the stock and receive no deduction relative to the income you reported at the time of the election.

Tax consequences of vesting. If you make the section 83b election, there is no tax consequence at the time the stock vests. Under this election you're treated as if the stock was vested when you acquired it, so there is nothing to report at the time it *actually* becomes vested.

Tax consequences at sale. You have the same tax consequences for a sale of stock after a section 83b election as if the stock had been vested when you received it. Your holding period begins on the date you received the stock, and your basis is the amount paid for the stock (if any), increased by the amount of compensation income you reported at that time.

Part VII provides more details concerning vesting and the section 83b election.

9

Planning for Restricted Stock

A little planning can improve your results from restricted stock awards or restricted stock units.

INVESTMENT PLANNING FOR RESTRICTED STOCK AWARDS and restricted stock units relates to the issue of managing risk. Most tax planning for this type of compensation revolves around vesting and the section 83b election. You can use these rules to change the year when you report the income, provided that you're willing to accept the other consequences. Some of these planning ideas require cooperation from the company. You should bear in mind that good tax planning for you may be bad tax planning for the company. Anything you do to reduce or postpone the amount of compensation income you have to report will cause a corresponding decrease or delay in the amount of compensation deduction the company will enjoy.

Risk management

The discussion of investment risk in Chapter 5 applies directly to stock you acquire through restricted stock awards and restricted stock units. In general, you shouldn't worry too much about these issues until the total value of your interests in the company (including stock options and company stock held in retirement accounts as well as stock you hold directly) becomes a significant part of your overall wealth. At lower levels, I believe it's generally best to hold onto the shares so you have at least a small investment in the company where you work.

When the overall dollar amount becomes large, you should think carefully about how to reduce your investment risk. The most obvious approach is to sell some of your shares. If that isn't possible, look for ways to reduce the risk level of your other investments. Avoid margin investing or other leverage (borrowing); make sure your stock investments are well diversified; consider shifting away from stocks to investments that expose you to less risk.

Some advisors promote *hedging* transactions to control risk. These arrangements use stock options or other "financial products" to offset losses you may suffer if your company's stock goes down. These transactions make sense in some cases, but overall I'm not a big fan, for reasons explained in Chapter 32.

Accelerating income

If you receive restricted stock units and your position with the company permits you to negotiate a different arrangement, you may want to consider whether you would be better off with a restricted stock award. In some circumstances you can improve on the tax consequences without really changing the deal.

We noted in Chapter 7 that a restricted stock award can be nearly the same as a restricted stock unit. One way you get the stock now, but it's held in escrow and you forfeit it if your employment terminates before the vesting date. The other way you don't receive the stock until the vesting date. The basic economics are the same if the company doesn't pay dividends, or if the restricted stock unit includes a right to receive substitute payments equivalent to any dividends paid during the vesting period. The restricted stock award may produce better tax treatment than the restricted stock unit, however, if you make the section 83b election. That would permit you to report compensation income at the time you receive the stock, rather than at the time the stock vests.

You would do this only if two things are true. First, you expect the value of the stock to go up during the vesting period. There's no point reporting income earlier than necessary just for the sake of paying taxes sooner. If you anticipate a price increase, though, you can use this maneuver to reduce the amount of compensation income you have to report. For shares that end up being held more than a year, the result is to convert the stock's appreciation from ordinary income into long-term capital gain, which is taxed at much lower rates. It may make sense to negotiate this change if you expect a big increase in the stock's value in the near future.

In addition, unless the value of the stock is very small when you receive it, you would want to be confident that your employment will last through the vesting period before heading in this direction. You wouldn't feel smart if you made this change, and paid taxes after filing the section 83b election, only to find that you end up forfeiting the stock.

> **Example:** Your employer offers to reward you with 2,000 shares of stock if you continue to work there another year. You feel that the value of the stock is likely to go up in that time, so you suggest an alternative: you'll receive the stock *now*, but *forfeit* it if you don't continue to work there another year. The company agrees. You receive the stock, make the section 83b election and pay tax on the current value.

Then the unexpected happens. You get an offer you can't refuse from another company. You quit your current job and forfeit the stock. Economically, you're in the same position as if you hadn't made the change, because you wouldn't have received the stock under the original deal. From a tax standpoint though, you're worse off, because you reported income when you made the section 83b election and you won't get any offsetting deduction when you forfeit the stock.

Deferring income

You can also use the rules for vesting to postpone income. Suppose your company is going to make a stock grant to you, without any restrictions. Normally that would mean you'll report compensation income, but you want to avoid reporting income this year. In this situation you might want to consider *asking* for a restriction on the stock, so that you'll forfeit it if your employment ends within the next year.

Naturally, you would do this only if you're confident that your employment will in fact continue for that period of time. You could be forfeiting a valuable right if you accept such a restriction and you leave your job. In addition, it wouldn't make sense to do this if you anticipate a great increase in the value of the stock while you're waiting for it to vest. These two possibilities—forfeiting the stock or seeing a hefty increase in its value before vesting—make delayed vesting a risky planning device. In limited circumstances, though, it makes sense to at least consider this approach.

You may be tempted to use a very short time period for the stock to vest. For example, if you're going to receive a stock grant in November, you may want to delay vesting until the beginning of January. This approach falls into a gray area, though. You can delay reporting compensation only if there is a *substantial risk of forfeiture.* The IRS might decide this wasn't *substantial.* There's no specific time period that's safe, but vesting that occurs less than six months after receipt of the stock seems questionable. Similarly, anything else you do to reduce or eliminate the risk that you'll forfeit the stock may cast doubt on whether the tax deferral will pass muster.

Benefits and risks of section 83b election

The section 83b election can provide multiple benefits. Most obviously, it reduces the amount of compensation income you have to report if the value of your stock goes up during the vesting period. It also starts the clock running sooner for long-term capital gains. This can be to your benefit even if the stock's value doesn't go up during the vesting period, assuming it goes up afterward and you sell it in the year following vesting.

> **Example:** You receive stock with vesting delayed by one year and make the section 83b election. A year later, the value is unchanged, so you didn't avoid any compensation income by making the election. But six months later the stock has gone up and you sell it. Because of the section 83b election, you'll report long-term capital gain. Without the election, your holding period would have started when the stock vested, and you would have had short-term capital gain when you sold the stock.

There's another benefit if the stock pays dividends. We mentioned earlier that dividends paid before the stock vests are treated as compensation income. If you make the section 83b election, you're treated as if you received vested shares. That means any dividends are eligible for the special 15% tax rate.

There's a downside to the election. For one thing, it requires you to pay tax earlier than would otherwise be necessary. All other things being equal, it's better to pay taxes later. You also have to consider the possibility the stock value will *fall* during the vesting period, in which case the election caused you to pay more tax than necessary. And then there's the possibility of a real disaster: paying tax after making the section 83b election and then forfeiting the stock. You didn't just pay tax sooner in this situation. You paid a tax you never would have had to pay at all!

There are some circumstances where you should definitely make the section 83b election. One is where you paid fair market value for the stock, but agreed to have it be subject to a restriction that prevents it from being vested. There's no cost at all to this election, and it can prevent you from having a painful tax bill at the time the stock vests. It's also a good idea to think about the section 83b election in situations where the value of the stock is very low at the time you receive it, and there's a possibility it will rise sharply before vesting. This is often the case when a company is planning to make an initial public offering (IPO).

Part III
Options in General

10

Options 101

Here are some basics that apply to all types of stock options.

A STOCK OPTION IS AN AGREEMENT providing terms under which you can buy a specified number of shares of stock at a specified price. Your option will increase in value as the company's stock grows. If the stock goes down instead, you won't reap value from your option but you won't have lost anything (other than the value of the option), because you aren't *required* to buy stock. A stock option is that free lunch you've been looking for: a chance to benefit from the upside without any risk of loss on the downside.

Option terminology

Stock options have their own lingo. Here are the basic terms you need to understand.

- **Grant or award.** You receive the stock option when the company makes a *grant* or *award*.

- **Vesting.** The option agreement or plan may say you can't use the option right away. The time you have to wait before using the option is the *vesting period.* An option is *vested* when you can use the option to buy stock.

- **Exercise.** You *exercise* an option when you notify the company that you want to purchase stock and provide payment according to the terms of the option.

- **Exercise price.** This is the price you pay if you decide to exercise the option. If you have an option to buy 100 shares at $15 per share, your exercise price is $15 per share. The exercise price is also sometimes called the *strike price,* the *striking price* or the *option price.*

- **Spread.** The difference between the current value of the stock and the strike price is the *spread.* If the current value of the stock is $20 and your option permits you to buy it at $15, the spread is $5 per share. The spread is also sometimes called the *bargain element.*

- **In the money.** An option is *in the money* when the spread is positive—in other words, when the value of the stock is higher than the exercise price.

- **Under water.** Options are *under water* (or *out of the money*) if the spread is negative; in other words, if the strike price is higher than the current value of the stock. There is no special tax significance to an option being under water, but the practical significance is that the option will not produce a profit until the stock price recovers.

- **Option agreement.** When a company grants an option, it should provide you with an *option agreement.* This document spells out the key terms of your option, including the number of shares you can buy, the purchase price, and the time periods during which you're permitted to exercise the option.

- **Prospectus.** An option is an opportunity to invest, so companies usually provide a *prospectus* when granting options. This is a summary of the terms of the option and other information intended to help you decide whether to exercise the option.

- **Stock option plan.** Options are usually (but not always) issued pursuant to a formal *stock option plan* adopted by the board of directors and approved by the shareholders. The stock option plan often provides additional details concerning the terms of your options. Don't confuse the stock option plan with a prospectus or other summary. In any situation where you need to know precisely what your rights are, you should obtain a copy of the plan.

Two kinds of stock options

Employee stock options come in two flavors: *nonqualified options* and *incentive stock options*. Employees can receive either kind or some of each. An option granted to a non-employee, such as an independent director or consultant, can't be an ISO, so if you aren't an employee you'll receive only nonqualified stock options.

Differences in tax treatment

Employees generally prefer incentive stock options. The special tax rules for ISOs are favorable to the holders of these options:

- You have to report income when you exercise a nonqualified option, but not when you exercise an incentive stock option.

- The income you report when you exercise a nonqualified option is compensation income. If you satisfy a special holding period requirement after exercising an incentive stock option, all your profit from the ISO will be long-term capital gain. You won't have to report any compensation income.

But ISOs bring bad news, too. When you exercise an incentive stock option, you're likely to have to pay alternative minimum tax (AMT). This tax may take away much of the benefit of not having to report income when you exercise your option. Apart from the cost of paying the tax, the complexity of dealing with the AMT can be daunting.

ISOs may be unattractive to employers for other reasons. Options don't qualify as incentive stock options unless they meet a list of requirements set forth in the Internal Revenue Code. Employers have more flexibility in dealing with nonqualified options. What's more, employers receive less favorable tax treatment for ISOs than for nonqualified options. The tax detriment to the company from choosing incentive stock options instead of nonqualified options may be greater than the tax benefit to the employee.

Which do you have?

Sometimes option holders are uncertain as to which type of option they have. This is the first thing you need to know! If you're unclear on this, here's how to find out.

Non-employees. If you're not an employee—in other words, you're not someone who has withholding taken from each paycheck and receives a W-2 at the end of the year—your option *has* to be a nonqualified option. The tax law doesn't permit companies to issue incentive stock options to non-employees. Even if your option says it's an ISO, it's a nonqualified option if you aren't an employee.

The option agreement. If you're an employee and unsure which type of option you have, the most reliable way to find the answer is to read the option agreement. You should have a copy of this document in your permanent records. If you don't, be sure to obtain a copy from the company.

- If the option agreement says the option is not an ISO, then that's your answer. Even if an option meets all other requirements to be an incentive stock option, the tax law says it's not an ISO if the option agreement declares that the option isn't an incentive stock option.

- If the option agreement says the option is an incentive stock option, then that *should* be your answer. Just saying that an option is an ISO isn't enough to make it one, however. The option has to satisfy a list of requirements in the tax law. For example, ISOs must be issued pursuant to a plan that has been approved by the company's shareholders. An incentive stock option can't be issued for a price that's lower than the fair market value of the stock on the date the option is granted, and can't extend for a period of more than 10 years. There are additional requirements, including special restrictions for individuals who own more than 10% of the stock of the company issuing the options.

Other rules. There are other rules that can change an incentive stock option to a nonqualified option. One is a $100,000 per year limit. This limit is based on the value of the stock at the time the option is granted, but it applies to the year the option *becomes exercisable*, not the year you receive the option or the year you actually exercise it.

> **Example:** You receive an incentive stock option that permits you to buy up to $400,000 worth of the company's stock. You can exercise one-fourth of the option immediately, but have to wait a year before exercising the second one-fourth, another year for the third one-fourth and one more year for the final one-fourth. This arrangement complies with the $100,000 limit, even if the stock is worth millions by the time you're eligible to exercise the last one-fourth.

The option described in the example consumes your entire limit for a four-year period. If you received any other options that became exercisable during that period, they would have to be nonqualified options.

Sometimes a company will issue options that exceed the limit without specifying that part of the option is a nonqualified option. That means you could have an option that *says* it's an ISO when in reality it's partly or entirely a nonqualified option. It's important to know how much of your option is nonqualified in this situation, because this will influence your tax planning.

Termination of employment. The tax law says an option isn't an ISO if you exercise it more than a limited period after your employment terminates: one year if employment terminates because of disability, otherwise three months. Your option, or the plan under which it's issued, may provide a *shorter* period. If your ISO remains exercisable for a *longer* period, its status as an ISO will terminate at the end of the three-month (or one-year) period.

Changing the agreement. Sometimes companies and option holders agree to change the terms of the options after they've been granted. If the option is an ISO, these changes have to be carefully reviewed. Some types of changes will be treated as a cancellation of the old option and issuance of a new one. The "new" option won't qualify as an incentive stock option if it doesn't meet all applicable requirements. In particular, it would be necessary to increase the exercise price if the value of the stock went up after the original issue date of the option. Great care is necessary whenever changing the terms of an incentive stock option that's already been issued.

More on option vesting

The words *vesting* and *vested* cause plenty of confusion. Partly this is because they're used differently depending on whether we're talking about *stock* or *stock options*. We say *stock* is vested at the point in time when you can quit your job and still keep the stock (or at least receive full value for it). Part VII of this book deals with various rules for vesting of stock.

We mean something different when we say an *option* is vested. An option becomes vested at the point in time when you can exercise it (use it to buy stock). You don't necessarily get to keep an option when you quit your job, even if the option is vested. Most options terminate when your employment terminates or shortly thereafter, perhaps with some added leeway if your employment ends due to death or disability.

> Your option may be exercisable even though the stock you buy under the option is *not* vested. If your company has an "early exercise" stock option plan (see Chapter 25), you may be in a position where you can exercise the option but you don't get to keep the stock if your employment terminates before a specified date.

The vesting rules for your stock option may appear in the option agreement or in the stock option plan. One of the first things you should do when you receive a stock option is determine when it becomes exercisable—in other words, when it vests. Many options vest gradually over a number of years.

Example: You receive an option with a ten-year term, permitting you to buy 120 shares of your company's stock at a specified price. The option has a four-year vesting schedule. For the first year you can't exercise any of the option. Beginning on the first anniversary of the grant date, you can buy up to 30 shares. When you reach the second anniversary of the grant date, you can buy another 30 shares. Vesting is cumulative, so if you didn't buy the first 30 shares yet, you're now eligible to buy 60 shares. After four years have gone by, you're eligible to buy all 120 shares. You can exercise the entire option then, or part of it, or wait until later.

How options are granted

Most nonqualified options, and *all* incentive stock options, are granted pursuant to a *stock option plan* that was adopted by the company's board of directors and approved by the shareholders. The board of directors, or a committee appointed by the board (usually called the *compensation committee*), may decide who receives the awards and the specific terms of the options. In some cases options are granted according to a formula set forth in the plan or in an employment agreement.

What you'll receive

When a company grants an option it should provide certain documents. You should receive an *option agreement*, setting forth the specific terms of your option. If the option is issued under a plan, you may also receive a copy of the plan, which provides some general rules that govern all options. In many cases the company provides a summary of the plan, called a *prospectus*.

These documents determine your rights as an option holder. Make sure you keep them in a safe place, and review them from time to time for planning purposes. At a minimum, think about your options before the end of each year to see if you want to exercise some or all of the options by December 31 as part of your tax planning.

> **Note:** It's a good idea to get a copy of the stock option plan if it's available, because this document can clarify your rights in some situations.

Typical terms

Companies have great flexibility in the terms they can offer for options. Your options may differ from the typical option in a number of important ways. Yet it may be helpful to compare your option with the norm:

- The exercise price is usually set at the value of the stock at the time the option is granted. For incentive stock options granted to anyone owning 10% or more of the company, the price has to be at least 110% of the fair market value of the stock when the option is granted.

- Typically, the option becomes exercisable over a period of several years. For example, you may be able to exercise 25% after one year, 50% after two years, and so on. Other schedules are possible.

- Cash payment is usually required at the time of exercise, but some companies make a form of "cashless exercise" available, where you borrow the exercise price from a broker and immediately sell enough shares to repay the loan.

- The option has an expiration date, which is often ten years after the date of grant, although some companies use a shorter period. For incentive stock options granted to anyone owning 10% or more of the company, the maximum period allowed is five years.

- The option expires earlier if employment terminates. You may or may not have a grace period (usually no more than three months) to exercise options at the time employment terminates. The grace period generally applies only to options that were exercisable when your employment terminated. Options that were scheduled to become exercisable on some later date typically expire when your employment ends, even if the date they would have become exercisable falls within the grace period. Some companies offer more generous terms if employment terminates as a result of normal retirement.

Bear in mind that these are merely the most typical terms. You should check your stock option agreement and other relevant documents to determine the actual terms of your own stock options.

Tax consequences of receiving an option

With rare exceptions, there's no tax to pay, and nothing to report, at the time you receive a nonqualified option. This is true even if the option is fully vested when you receive it. The exceptions:

- You receive an option that's actively traded on an established securities market, or virtually identical to options that are actively traded. That's possible in theory but never happens in practice.

- You receive a nonqualified option that's in the money at the time you receive it.

Before 2005, you could receive a nonqualified stock option that was in the money when granted, with no adverse tax consequences unless the option was "deep in the money" (for example, a $2 option to buy shares worth $40). Under a tax law passed in 2004 (section 409A) you may have adverse tax consequences on the grant date or, if later, the vesting date, if your option is even slightly in the money at the time it's granted. Companies rarely grant options that are in the money, so you almost never have to worry about reporting income when you receive a grant.

No section 83b election

There's persistent confusion among taxpayers—and even among some tax professionals—about the section 83b election. This election can provide tax savings when you receive *stock* that's not vested. But the election doesn't apply when you receive an *option*. You may hear that there's an election you can make to reduce your tax when you receive a nonqualified option, but that's a mistake. The section 83b election is for stock only.

The election can be used in connection with "early exercise" options that are sometimes offered by pre-IPO companies, but only when you *exercise* the option. See Chapter 25.

No tax when option becomes exercisable

Most options aren't immediately exercisable. Usually you're permitted to exercise the option only if you continue to work for the company for a stated period.

Example: You receive an option to buy 300 shares of the company's stock, but you're not permitted to exercise the option immediately. If you're still employed with that company a year later you become eligible to exercise half of this option. After another year of employment the option is fully exercisable.

The dates on which the option becomes exercisable are significant, but you don't report income on these dates. The tax law takes no notice of them.

Option planning starts now

Planning for your options should begin the day you receive them. Begin by understanding your rights under the agreement and the stock option plan. Read these documents carefully, and make sure you can answer these questions:

- What is the earliest date you can exercise the option? Does it become exercisable in stages?

- What do you need to do when you exercise the option? Can you borrow to exercise the option? Can you pay the exercise price using stock you already own?

- What restrictions will be imposed on the stock you receive when you exercise the option? Can you sell it right away if you want to? Transfer it to a trust or family partnership?

Does the company have the right to get the stock back under any circumstances?

- When will the option terminate? Can you exercise after your employment terminates? What if you die while holding the option?

Start thinking *now* about how and when you'll exercise the options. Will you exercise them all at once, or in stages over a number of years? What scenario will provide the best result for you? How will you come up with the money to exercise the options? And the money to pay the taxes? How will you handle an unexpected situation, such as loss of your job?

How to exercise a stock option

Later in this book we'll talk about *when* to exercise options, and what your tax consequences will be. Before that knowledge can do you any good, you need to know *how* to exercise a stock option.

Step 1: Know your rights. To start with, you need to know whether you can exercise any of your stock options, and if so, which ones. When in doubt, read your option agreement and relevant parts of the stock option plan. If you don't have copies of these documents, you should be able to obtain them from the company.

You may find that you can exercise some of your stock options but not others. As indicated above, you may be able to exercise only *part* of a stock option. Even if your stock options are fully exercisable, you may wish to exercise only part of an option. Most plans permit partial exercise, subject to a minimum amount.

Example: A typical provision might say you can exercise part of an option, but no fewer than ten shares at a time unless that's all you have at the time you exercise.

Step 2: Select a stock option. You may find that you have more than one stock option that's available for exercise. Unless you're planning to exercise all your options at once, you need to choose which stock option to exercise.

> **Example:** You hold an option to buy 100 shares at $18 per share, and another option to buy 200 shares at $15 per share. Both stock options are fully exercisable. You want to exercise for 100 shares.

The easy thing to do is to exercise the option for 100 shares at $18. But if your plan permits (as most do), you can exercise half of the other option instead. That would cost $300 less because of the lower exercise price, but cause you to report an additional $300 of income.

Step 3: Select a method of payment. In the bad old days there was only one way to pay for stock when you exercised an option. In legal mumbo-jumbo, you had to *tender readily available funds.* In other words, you had to come up with cash.

That's still a popular method of payment, but some companies now make other alternatives available. The company may have an arrangement with a stock broker under which some or all of the stock is sold immediately to cover the exercise price and any tax withholding. See below for a discussion of *cashless exercise.*

Another possibility is to use stock you already own to pay the exercise price. For example, if it will cost $2,000 to exercise your option, you can turn in $2,000 worth of stock instead of $2,000 in cash. Not all companies offer this alternative. You may achieve benefits with this form of exercise that aren't available when you pay cash. Due to the complexity involved, Part VI of this book devotes several chapters to this form of exercise.

Step 4: Withholding. If you're an employee and you exercise a nonqualified option, the company has to withhold on the income you receive from exercising the option. Usually that means you have to come up with additional cash besides the option price. Before you exercise your option, you should determine what your withholding obligation will be and how you'll meet it. The precise dollar amount won't be determined until you exercise the option, because the amount of income (and therefore the amount of withholding) is based on the value of the stock on the day you exercise.

Step 5: Exercise the option. Now you know exactly what you want to do and you're ready to exercise the option. Once again you have to look at the option agreement and the stock option plan to learn how to proceed. Most larger companies have a form you must fill out when you exercise an option, or even a way to exercise online. Other companies simply require notification in writing. In that case you would write a brief letter or memo something like this:

> *In accordance with my option agreement dated September 10, 2005 I hereby exercise my option to purchase 120 shares of common stock at the price of $30 per share. My check in the amount of $3,600 is attached.*

Chances are you won't be the first person to exercise an option at your company. If you're in doubt as to how to proceed, contact the appropriate office for instructions.

Cashless exercise

Some employers make it easier for option holders to exercise their options by providing a way to combine the exercise of the option with a sale of some or all of the stock. In this situation you don't have to come up with any money to exercise the option or pay any withholding. That's why we call this a *cashless exercise* of your option.

Usually the company makes arrangements with a brokerage firm, which loans the money needed to buy the stock. The brokerage firm sells some or all of the stock immediately, with part of the sale proceeds being used to repay the loan as soon as the cash becomes available. Another part of the sale proceeds will be used to cover any withholding requirement that applies, and any brokerage commissions and other fees. You receive whatever is left in the form of cash (if you sold all the shares) or unsold shares (if you sold only some of the shares).

> The term *sell to cover* is sometimes used for a transaction where you sell just enough shares to cover the cost of exercising the option.

Not all companies permit cashless exercise. Some companies want to encourage option holders to retain the stock so they'll have an ongoing stake in the business. Others may be concerned that sales executed in this manner will depress the price of their stock. Review your option documents, or check with the company, to see if this method of exercising your options is available.

Tax consequences. The tax consequences of a cashless exercise are the same as if you took two separate steps: exercising the option, then selling the stock. You don't get different tax treatment as a result of combining the steps. Tax consequences of exercising an option and selling shares are covered in later chapters.

Frequently asked questions. Most confusion in this area comes when people don't realize that the single act of choosing a cashless exercise has to be reported as two transactions.

> **Q:** My gain from exercising the option appears on my Form W-2 as wages—but Form 1099-B reports the full amount of proceeds, including the gain. Why is the same amount reported twice?
>
> **A:** The same amount is *reported* twice, but it isn't *taxed* twice. Form 1099-B shows how much you received for selling the stock. When you figure your gain or loss, the amount reported on your W-2 is treated as an additional amount paid for the stock. (In other words, it increases your *basis*.) The effect is to reduce your gain or increase your loss, so you're not double taxed.
>
> **Q:** Why do I have gain or loss when the stock was sold at the same time I exercised?

A: Often there's a gain or loss to report, for two reasons. First, the amount reported on your W-2 as income may be based on the stock's average price for the day you exercised your option, but the broker may have sold at a price slightly (or more than slightly) above or below that average price. And second, your sale proceeds are likely to be reduced by a brokerage commission and other costs, which can produce a small loss.

> The IRS does not require Form 1099-B in some cases where you sell shares the same day you exercise the option, but you still have to report the sale on your tax return.

Can my IRA exercise my option?

You pay taxes, your IRA doesn't. That simple fact may lead you to the idea of having your IRA exercise your options. If it worked, you would get the benefit of the economic bargain inherent in your options, while the tax consequences would be deferred until you draw money from your IRA.

Unfortunately, options and IRAs don't mix. Regardless of whether you have nonqualified options or ISOs, you can't use your IRA to exercise options you received as compensation. The main problem here is that you would have to transfer your option to the IRA. Your IRA can't exercise an option it doesn't own. Yet the tax laws prohibit you from transferring anything other than cash to an IRA except in a qualified rollover. If this idea occurred to you as a way to handle your options, give yourself credit for creativity—and then move on to other ideas.

Stock Option Economics

An understanding of stock option economics can help you make informed decisions about your compensation package and your stock option strategy.

STOCK OPTIONS ARE FULL OF CONTRADICTIONS. They are both simple and complicated. They are a no-lose proposition and a high-risk investment. This chapter sorts out the contradictions so you can understand the economics of your stock options.

A risk-free investment

A stock option provides a way for you to profit from the performance of your company's stock without putting any of your money at risk. Here are three key facts about how they work:

1. If the stock is trading at a price higher than the exercise price, you can make a profit by exercising the option and selling the shares.

2. You don't have to exercise the option if the stock value is lower than the exercise price.

3. You didn't pay anything for the option, so there's no out of pocket loss if you simply allow the option to lapse.

It's easy to see that your profit from the option (on paper, at least) is $1 per share for every dollar the stock value rises above the exercise price. For example, if your option gives you the right to buy 500 shares at a price of $20 per share, a market price of $24 per share would correspond to a paper profit of $2,000 (500 shares times a profit of $4 per share).

At the option's expiration date, you'll let it lapse if the stock value is at or below the exercise price. That means you don't care *how far* below the exercise price the final stock value might be. If the stock value is *above* the exercise price, you'll exercise the option, and in that case it certainly *does* matter how far above that price the stock value has risen.

> Options provide profit equal to the difference between the stock value and the exercise price, with no loss on a stock value below that price.

In this description of the *profit profile* of a stock option, you can see that an option is, in a sense, a no-lose proposition. You either make a profit (when the stock price goes up) or you break even (when the stock price stays the same or goes down). I've heard of people refusing stock options offered by their employer, and I have to assume they're confused about this point. There's never any reason to turn down an offer of stock options because they represent a potential profit with no risk of loss.

A high-risk investment

If there's no risk of loss, how can a stock option be a high-risk investment? The answer is that the option itself has value—sometimes a great deal of value—and that value can rapidly disappear. You worked hard to earn your stock options, and deserve whatever profits you can obtain from them. Exercising your options too soon or too late, or making other mistakes in handling your stock or options, may cause you to suffer a painful economic loss. If you see a great deal of wealth disappear in a short period of time, it may not be much consolation to know you didn't lose any money out of pocket.

Earlier, we described options as investments on steroids. They can gain value much more rapidly than an investment in shares of stock, and lose value just as quickly. That's mainly because options have built-in leverage. In Chapter 5 we talked about leverage that comes from borrowing money to make investments. The same concept applies to stock options because they provide you with a way to delay paying for shares of stock, even though you're already getting a benefit from any increase in the stock's value. It's almost like getting an interest-free loan.

When it comes to stock options, the built-in leverage is both good and bad. It supercharges your profit potential, but also exposes you to a risk that your profits will disappear. That's one reason it's so difficult to decide when to cash in your profits. We'll provide an approach that balances risk and reward.

Importance of option value

Option holders need to understand the *value* of their stock options. There are at least three situations where the information can be useful: taking a new job, leaving an old job, and deciding when to exercise your stock options.

Taking a new job. When you're considering a job offer that includes stock options, you'd like to know what the options are worth. This is especially true if you have offers from more than one company. Options that are worth $5,000 might influence your decision one way. The prospect of receiving options worth $50,000 could have a different impact on your thinking.

Leaving an old job. If your existing job provides you with stock options, chances are that you'll leave some of that value behind if you terminate your employment. Sometimes people abandon options that have a great deal of value without realizing it. If you learn that $100,000 of option value will go up in smoke when you quit, it might put a different light on whether you can put up with your current boss for a while longer.

When to exercise your stock options. In the next chapter we'll see how option value plays a role in deciding when to exercise a stock option.

Understanding option value

Before we can discuss option value we need to know what we *mean* by option value. Many option holders think of their options as having a value equal to the current "paper profit" based on the value of the stock. Ask about the value of their options and they'll give you a number that represents the built-in profit based on the current trading price of the stock. For a brand new option (before the stock price has gone up) they might say it isn't worth anything yet.

> **Example:** Your option allows you to buy 800 shares of stock at $12.50 per share, and the stock is currently trading at $15.00. The option has a built-in profit of $2.50 per share, and this profit applies to 800 shares, for a total built-in profit of 800 times $2.50, or $2,000.

The built-in profit is certainly an important number, and we have a special name for it: it's called the *intrinsic value* of a stock option. You can calculate it quite easily by subtracting the exercise price of your option from the current market value of the stock. The intrinsic value of the option goes up and down in a direct relationship with the trading price of the stock. Yet intrinsic value never drops below zero, because you don't have to exercise the option if the stock is trading at a price below the exercise price of the option. Intrinsic value is always either zero or a positive number.

It's important—*really* important—to understand that intrinsic value is only part of the value of your stock options. To see what we're getting at, consider what price you would accept if you had a chance to sell your options. You aren't likely to have this opportunity because nearly all companies forbid sales of the options they grant to their employees. Yet we get a better picture of the value of your options if we ask the hypothetical question: what price would you accept if you *could* sell them? We don't get a very good answer if we rely solely on the built-in profit, or intrinsic value.

> **Example:** Your option allows you to buy 800 shares of stock at $12.50 per share. The stock is trading at $12.55, and the option doesn't expire for another four years. The option has a built-in profit of $0.05 per share, and this profit applies to 800 shares. The intrinsic value of the option is 800 times $0.05, or $40.

Would you be willing to sell this option for $40? Not likely. We saw earlier that the same option will produce a profit of $2,000 if the stock price goes up to $15.00. We don't have any assurance that the stock price *will* go that high, but it seems like a reasonable possibility, considering that the expiration date is four years away. The opportunity to get that kind of profit, or possibly an even greater profit, is surely worth more than $40.

Common sense tells you the option has a value far greater than its intrinsic value. You can't always rely on common sense in dealing with stock options, but in this case it is pointing you in the right direction. You would be foolish to sell the option for $40 when it could easily provide you with a profit of thousands of dollars.

How about $400? Or $4,000? At some point we reach a price where it would make sense to sell the option. The precise number is far from obvious, but it's clear that the number has to include something more than the intrinsic value. The additional value represents the profit potential from continuing to hold the stock option. The size of this profit potential depends in part on the amount of time left until the option expires, so we call it the *time value* of the option.

> The overall value of a stock option includes the intrinsic value, representing built-in profit, and the time value, representing the value of potential profit.

More about option value

It's easy to see how to determine intrinsic value: you simply subtract the exercise price of the option from the current value. Time value is more elusive. How can we put a value on the potential profit of a stock option, when we don't know how much profit it will produce? For all we know, the stock could double in value, and double again, so your options are worth a small fortune—or the stock price could plummet, making your options worthless.

Experts in finance solved this problem using statistical methods. They came up with something called the *Black-Scholes formula*. In essence, this complicated formula calculates the average profit from holding a stock option, where the average is weighted according to the probabilities of each possible outcome. Option traders use this formula to determine the price when they buy or sell stock options. The result doesn't tell you how much profit you'll get from any particular stock option, but in theory it tells you the *average* outcome for a stock option with these characteristics.

I want to stress this point: *an option's value is not a prediction of the outcome.* Instead, it's an *average* of the possible outcomes. This average includes situations where options produce huge profits and other situations where they produce no profit at all. It would be pure coincidence if your option ended up producing a profit equal to the value that was calculated earlier.

I've heard people make statements like this: "They calculated the value of my stock options, but the value turned out to be wrong." That shows a misunderstanding of option value. The speaker is treating the value of the option as a prediction. The value isn't a prediction, so it can't "turn out to be wrong."

The value is still useful information, though. It gives you an intelligent way to evaluate this part of your compensation package, and it can help you make good decisions about how to handle your stock option. Just don't fall into the trap of thinking it's a prediction.

> Your option's value is a useful piece of information, but it doesn't tell you how much profit you'll make from the option.

Factors affecting value

Formulas that determine the value of stock options have to take into account at least six different factors. We won't cover them in detail, but two of them deserve special attention.

Dividends. Many people feel that it's a good idea to hold stocks that pay dividends. Yet dividends *reduce* the value of a stock option. That's because option holders don't receive dividends until they exercise the option and hold the stock. In most of the discussion here we assume the company doesn't pay dividends. If your company pays dividends, your option values are lower than they would be if the company retained all its earnings, or used earnings to repurchase shares.

Volatility. Here's another factor that may seem to be upside-down. *Volatility* refers to how much a stock zigzags up and down. It's a way to measure risk: stocks with high volatility have more risk of loss than stocks with low volatility. Yet volatility *increases* the value of a stock option. That's because a big upward swing in the stock price can produce a big profit. Big downward swings don't hurt an option holder the way they hurt a stockholder, because you won't exercise the option when it's under water.

When the experts use a formula to determine the value of a stock option, volatility is one of the most important factors. Yet I'm inclined to discount the value of high volatility for people like you, holding employee stock options. It's an advantage in figuring the theoretical value of a stock option but a disadvantage because it exposes you to a high level of risk. When determining the value an option has *to you*, I recommend using a moderate figure for volatility (no more than 30%), even if the actual volatility of your company's stock is higher.

Value of a newly issued option

The value of a newly issued option can be important information if you're evaluating a job offer, or simply trying to determine whether the compensation package of your current employer is adequate. Some companies calculate the value of your options and provide that information at the time of the option grant. Others leave it up to you to figure out what your stock options are worth.

If you work for a company that has publicly traded stock, an expert can determine the value of the option according to valuation theory. Yet there's a simpler way to determine your option's value without the help of an expert:

Multiply the value of the stock times 30%.

Example: You receive an option to buy 2,000 shares at $30 per share. The total stock value is $60,000 (2,000 shares times $30). Under our simplified formula, the value of this option at the time it is granted is 30% of that amount, or $18,000.

Sound too simple? It's good enough for most purposes. In fact, the number you get this way is arguably more appropriate than the number you would get from an expert valuation of your stock option. An expert valuation tells you the theoretically correct value of a stock option in an ideal world where you're free to sell your option to the highest bidder. We're trying to determine a value that's appropriate for an option that can't be sold and probably doesn't represent an ideal investment for your portfolio. That allows us to take certain liberties.

For one thing, we're disregarding any value that's added by having an option extend beyond five years. Your option may be for six years, or eight, or ten, but the odds are pretty good that you'll either choose to exercise it within five years or have a change in employment that *forces* you to exercise (or abandon) it within that time. I feel that the added value of holding an employee stock option more than five years from now is too speculative to take into account.

We're also disregarding the value of high volatility. As explained above, the theoretical value of a stock option is higher for stocks that zigzag more than others. Yet this higher volatility also exposes you to more risk. When we determine the value of an option *to you*, high volatility is a positive factor and a negative factor. The advantage and disadvantage tend to cancel each other out, so for our purposes it's reasonable to use the same value for a high volatility option as for a moderate volatility option.

> If someone determines your options are worth much more than this figure, they are probably attributing value to a time period greater than five years or to a relatively high volatility.

Reducing the value. We can refine our 30% formula somewhat. If your company's stock pays dividends, you might shade it down somewhat, perhaps to 25%. If it pays dividends at a high rate (more than 1% of the stock value each year), reduce it even more. If you doubt that you'll stick around at the company long enough for your options to vest, you should discount the value for that uncertainty as well.

Using the formula. This simple formula provides a way to compare apples and oranges. If one prospective employer offers a pay package that includes stock worth $20,000, and the other offers a package that includes an option to buy stock worth $60,000, you can consider these two offerings to be roughly equivalent, because our formula give a value of $18,000 for the option. For another example, suppose your company says you won't be getting a $10,000 bonus you were expecting, but they'll replace it with an option to buy stock worth $50,000. You might prefer to receive the bonus, but they replaced it with an option of greater value so you'll know they've made a good faith effort to make up for the missing cash.

Value of older options

After the stock price moves up or down it becomes harder to determine the value of a stock option. Some companies provide an easy way to determine that value, perhaps as part of an online statement. Just be sure you're looking at overall option value, and not just the intrinsic value (the built-in profit). A professional advisor with access to appropriate software may be able to provide the value if it isn't available from your company. Unfortunately, the Black-Scholes formula is so complicated that it probably doesn't make sense for you to use it to value your options, even if you can locate an online calculator designed for this purpose. The following thoughts may be helpful in thinking about option value in situations where a professionally calculated number isn't readily available.

Underwater options. Your company's stock may go down after you receive your stock options, and in that case your options are *under water*. For example, you may receive an option to buy stock at $12 per share only to see the market price drop to $10. The option won't produce a profit for you until the stock price climbs back to a level above $12, and that could take a long time.

Option holders have a tendency to discount the value of underwater stock options more than they should. If the option still has a long enough time to go before it expires, it can have a surprisingly high value even though the market price of the stock seems stuck at a level below the exercise price. If you're thinking of leaving your job because your options are under water, find out what those options are truly worth. You may learn that these seemingly worthless options have a great deal of value.

> As an example, an option to buy stock at $12 per share, valued when the stock is trading at $10 (so the option is $2 under water), can easily have a Black-Scholes value of $3 per share or more.

Options that are in the money. It's more pleasant to contemplate the value of an option that's in the money. Remember that the value is divided into two parts: intrinsic value and time value. Intrinsic value is simply the built-in profit, so that's easy to calculate. Just subtract the exercise price of the option from the current price of the stock.

Time value is more difficult to determine. That's where an option valuation formula comes in. These formulas tell you the *total* value of your option (intrinsic value plus time value). If you want to know the time value, take the overall value of the option and subtract the intrinsic value. The next chapter will show how this information can be useful in determining when to exercise your stock options.

Even without using an option valuation formula you can get a pretty good idea what your options are worth when they're in the money. It's easy to calculate intrinsic value, and you can estimate time value close enough for most purposes. Here's how.

First, recall that we said a brand new option should be valued at 30% of the stock value. That's an option with zero intrinsic value (the stock price hasn't had a chance to move), so the option has only time value. It turns out that time value doesn't go up when the stock price goes up. In fact, it goes down somewhat. So time value will always be 30% or less of the *original* value of the stock. (Remember, we're ignoring the value of option life beyond five years and any added value for high volatility, so the value we're using may be lower than the value an expert would calculate.) If you're valuing an option that's in the money, you'll get a reasonable estimate of the time value if you start with 25% of the original stock value and reduce it proportionately if the option will expire in less than five years.

> **Example:** Your option lets you buy stock at $15 per share and the stock is trading at $25. The option expires in four years. The intrinsic value is easy: $10 per share. To determine the time value, we start with 25% of the original stock value and reduce that number by one-fifth because the option expires in four years. In other words, we multiply the original value of $15 times 20% to get a time value of $3 per share. The total value of the option is $13 per share ($10 intrinsic value and $3 time value).

The value you get using this procedure is a rough estimate, but serves well for planning purposes. If you need a more precise number, you'll need to get the option value from your company or from a professional advisor as discussed earlier.

12

When to Exercise an Option

There are at least five different approaches people use in
deciding when to exercise their stock options, but most of
them aren't valid.

THE TIME TO EXERCISE is one of the most important decisions
you'll make about your stock options, and also one of the most
difficult. Even the experts have a hard time with this question. We're
going to look at some of the most common mistakes in dealing with
this issue, and show how to avoid them.

> As usual, we assume your company's stock is publicly traded. Some
> of the discussion here doesn't apply to privately held companies
> (see Chapter 28).

Outer limits

There are limits on when you can exercise, and also limits on when
you *should* exercise. Here's a brief rundown:

- You can't exercise your options until they're *vested*; in other words, you have to wait at least until the time specified in the option agreement.

- You can't exercise your option after it expires, either by passage of time or for some other reason (usually termination of employment).

- It may be permissible to exercise your option when it's under water, but that's a foolish move if you can buy the shares more cheaply in the stock market.

The time period we're concerned about is from the time your option becomes vested until the time it expires. That can be a period of many years, and a lot can happen in that time. People have seen their options go from zero intrinsic value to where they have a paper profit of millions, and back down to zero intrinsic value. How can you know the best time to exercise your options?

A general principle

You may find yourself in a position where you can either continue to hold an option or exercise it now and hold the stock. Normally it's better to continue holding the option if you plan to continue your investment. In other words, exercise the option only when you're ready to cash out by selling the stock (possibly after a one-year holding period if it's an incentive stock option) or when the option is about to expire.

One reason is that a stock option provides a form of downside protection you don't have when you hold shares of stock. If the stock price falls below the exercise price of the option, you don't lose any money because you don't have to exercise the option. Once you hold the shares, you're exposed to the full consequences of a collapse in the stock price.

Exercising the option sooner than necessary can hurt in other ways. You give up the opportunity to delay paying the exercise price, and in many cases you also give up the opportunity to delay paying taxes.

> In most cases where you have a choice, it's best to delay exercising your option until you're ready to sell the shares.

Five ways to choose

Here are five approaches people use to decide when to exercise their options. We'll follow up with a critique.

- Determine how the stock is most likely to perform. If the stock seems likely to go up, continue to hold the option. Exercise the option and sell the shares when the stock seems likely to go down.

- Exercise the option and sell the stock as soon as possible after the option becomes exercisable, assuming the option is in the money at that time.

- Hold the option as long as possible, exercising only at the time it is about to expire.

- Hold the option through most of its life, but exercise some period of time before it expires, such as two or three years.

- Exercise the option and sell the stock when the benefit of diversification outweighs the benefit of holding the option for a longer period.

The first four approaches can be wasteful or dangerous. The last one provides a valid way to determine when to exercise your stock options.

Timing based on stock performance

Many option holders base their decision on the likely performance of the company's stock. What could be more logical? It's obvious that you'll end up with more money if you continue to hold your option when the stock is going up, and exercise and sell before it goes down.

Unfortunately, as we saw in Chapter 4, it simply isn't possible to make a reliable prediction about the price of your company's stock. The information provided by stock analysts may be useful when building a diversified portfolio but can be dead wrong when it comes to any one stock. Likewise, the knowledge you gain about your company by going to work there every day doesn't help you predict how the stock is going to perform. The stock can go down when your company seems to be doing great, and it can go up when it seems to be in a rut. Your inside information is more likely to hurt than help, blinding you to realities that are apparent to objective observers.

A stock option strategy that is built on the predicted performance of the stock is a house built on sand. A sound strategy is one that takes into account the fundamental unpredictability of stock prices.

The "ASAP" strategy

If you take to heart my warnings against trying to foretell your company's stock price, you may be tempted to adopt another poor strategy: exercising your options as soon as possible. The idea is to get your profit off the table before it can disappear. This approach protects any paper profit you have at the time your option becomes exercisable, but it can be terribly wasteful.

Recall that your stock option has two kinds of value: intrinsic value, representing the built-in, paper profit, and time value, representing the value of potential profit from continuing to hold the option. When you exercise your stock option, you cash in the intrinsic value, and the remaining time value disappears. If you exercise sooner than necessary, you're abandoning part of the value of your stock option.

The intrinsic value of an option can be 20% or less of the option's value. If you exercise the option when that's true, you're destroying at least four times as much value as you're protecting. You've done a good job of preventing your paper profit from disappearing, but in many cases the price you paid is far too high.

The "bitter end" strategy

These observations could lead you to adopt the opposite strategy: wait until the option is about to expire. That's the only time you can exercise the option without destroying value, because the option always has at least some time value prior to expiration. This is the strategy for people who can't bring themselves to throw out a tube of toothpaste, because there's always just a little more if you squeeze hard enough.

This strategy avoids wasting the time value of your stock option, but may expose you to excessive investment risk. We saw in Chapter 5 that the risk of investing in a single stock can be several times as high as the risk in a diversified portfolio. The risk in a stock option is even higher than the risk in a single stock, because it includes leverage risk (the same kind of risk that comes from borrowing money to make investments). Up to a point, it's a good idea to continue holding your stock option rather than abandon the remaining time value. The time comes, however, when it's more important to protect your paper profit from SDS: sudden disappearance syndrome.

These observations highlight what I call the *optionee's dilemma*. You have to destroy part of your wealth to protect the other part. Determining when to exercise your option is a balancing act. You have to decide when the benefit of protecting the existing paper profit is important enough to justify abandoning the potential profit from continuing to hold the option.

When to use this strategy. Although the "bitter end strategy" isn't generally advisable, there are times when it makes perfectly good sense. If your options represent a small fraction of your wealth, and the rest of it is well diversified so that you don't have too much risk, you can continue holding your options until they're ready to expire. My warnings about risk apply to your overall net worth. If your options represent a thin sliver of the total, a decline in their value won't do major harm to your finances. Holding them until they're about to expire will allow you to take full advantage of the time value without incurring too much risk.

Even if your options represent a major portion of your net worth, you shouldn't focus too much on risk if you're just starting out and haven't built much wealth. For example, if you have $5,000 worth of stock options, $5,000 in a 401k account, and little else, don't lose sleep over the ideal time to exercise your stock options. They may represent 50% of your wealth right now, but that's a tiny fraction of the wealth you'll build as your career moves forward.

> Risk becomes important when your options represent both a large dollar amount and a large fraction of your total wealth.

The E minus strategy

People who understand the optionee's dilemma sometimes recommend a strategy where you exercise your stock options close to the end of their term, but not at the very end. For example, they might suggest exercising your options two or three years before they expire. We're subtracting a period of time from the expiration date, so I call this the *E minus strategy*.

The main idea here is to balance between your two concerns: protecting your existing paper profit without giving up too much of the potential for additional profit. Yet this is a crude way to address this issue. As we're about to see, there are times when the E minus strategy makes you exercise your options too soon, and other times when it makes you hold your options long after you should have exercised them to reduce your investment risk.

A well-balanced approach

Stated simply, the best time to exercise a stock option is when the advantages of doing so outweigh the disadvantages. As a general rule, the advantage comes from an opportunity to reduce or eliminate the investment risk involved in having your wealth fluctuate according to the value of a single company's stock. The disadvantage comes from giving up the potential for added wealth if you continue to hold the option. We want an approach that balances the two. I'll describe the theory, and then give you an easy way to apply this approach.

Recall our earlier discussion of intrinsic value and time value. When you exercise a stock option, you cash in the intrinsic value and abandon the remaining time value. A well-balanced approach is one in which you'll exercise your stock option when the benefit of protecting the paper profit built up in your stock option (in other words, the intrinsic value) outweighs the disadvantage of abandoning the remaining time value.

This doesn't mean you should exercise your option as soon as the intrinsic value is greater than the remaining time value. You don't necessarily want to abandon $50,000 in time value to protect $55,000 in paper profit. Balancing means making an informed judgment about the point when you gain an overall advantage by cashing in. Where you draw the line depends on your overall financial condition and, to some extent, on how comfortable you are with risk. What's more, in a balanced approach you don't have to exercise the entire option at one time.

Example: Your option has built up an intrinsic value of $140,000 and has a remaining time value of $60,000. If

$140,000 is a large fraction of your net worth, it probably makes sense to exercise at least part of the option and invest the proceeds in a way that reduces your risk. Yet the remaining time value is large enough so it would be reasonable to retain part of the option rather than exercising it all at once.

Why the E minus strategy fails. The E minus strategy seems to be designed to achieve this kind of balance, but in many cases it fails miserably. In some cases, the intrinsic value of a stock option is a tiny fraction of the overall value, even when the option has two years or less remaining before it expires. For example, you could hold an option to buy stock at $20 per share when the stock is trading at $21. With two years left to run, the time value of this option would be far greater than the puny $1 per share intrinsic value.

On the other hand, it's possible for an option to build up a paper profit that far exceeds its remaining time value when it still has five years or more to run. For example, if the stock value quickly triples from $20 to $60, the built-in profit is $40 per share and the time value is only about $5 per share. It could make perfectly good sense to exercise this option now, even though it won't expire for another five years or more. The time value you abandon is a small fraction of the built-in profit you can protect by exercising the option.

The E minus strategy incorrectly assumes there's a fixed point in time when the benefit of protecting the intrinsic value of your stock option outweighs the remaining time value.

Making it simple. We've looked at a lot of theory but the bottom line is pretty simple. If your company's stock price is a lot higher than the exercise price of your stock option, chances are that the built-in profit is far greater than the remaining time value. The option is ripe for harvesting, even if it won't expire for several years. On the other hand, if the stock price is only slightly higher than the exercise price of the option, it usually makes sense to delay exercising unless you're close to the time when your option will expire.

Part IV
Nonqualified Stock Options

13

Tax Rules for Nonqualified Stock Options

In most cases you'll report compensation income when you exercise a nonqualified stock option. Any additional profit when you sell the stock will be capital gain.

WE SAW IN CHAPTER 10 that you don't have to report any income when you receive a stock option, or when it becomes exercisable. That's one of the nice things about stock options: they let you build wealth while postponing tax liability. The general rule for this type of option is that you trigger a tax bill when you exercise the option. There's an exception we'll talk about later, for situations where the stock isn't vested at the time you exercise the option. Until then we're assuming your stock is vested at the time of exercise, which is true in the vast majority of cases.

How much income

When you exercise your nonqualified stock option, you have to report income equal to the bargain element of the option at the time of exercise. In other words, the amount of income is equal to the difference between the value of the stock and the amount you pay to exercise the option.

> **Example:** If you pay $8,000 to exercise a nonqualified stock option for $20,000 worth of stock, you'll report $12,000 of income.

Different companies have different methods for determining the value of the stock. Some use the average of the high and low selling price on the date of exercise; others may use the previous day's closing price or some other similar measure.

Here's a key point: the amount of income is fixed on the date you exercise the option, even if you don't sell the shares that day. A later change in the value of the stock won't change the amount of income you have to report. You have to report this income even if you end up selling the shares at a much lower price.

Compensation vs. capital gain

If you've held your stock option for a while before exercising it, you may wonder if you can treat your profit as capital gain. That's not allowed. Your profit from exercising the option is considered compensation income. If you have additional profit when you sell the shares, you'll treat that profit as capital gain.

> **Example:** You exercise a $12 option to buy 1,000 shares when the stock is trading at $18. After holding the shares for a while, you sell them at $22. You report $6,000 of compensation income on the exercise of the option (1,000 shares times $6 per share spread) and $4,000 of capital gain

when you sell the shares (1,000 shares times the additional $4 per share profit).

You can't change this result by making the section 83b election when you receive your stock option. As explained in Chapter 8, this election allows you to report income when you receive shares of stock that aren't vested. You can't file the election when you receive an *option*, though. Profits that build up before you exercise a nonqualified stock option are always compensation income, not capital gain.

If you're an employee, withholding and social security tax apply to your compensation income. Normally this means you have to come up with additional cash (on top of the exercise price) when you exercise your stock option. Bear in mind that the actual tax rate on this income may be higher than the withholding rate, so you may owe additional tax on April 15. Plan ahead so you're certain to have this money available when you need it.

If you're a non-employee (such as a consultant), you won't face withholding but you still have to treat this profit as compensation for services, not capital gain. That means you'll owe self-employment tax on top of income tax. In the worst case, your overall tax, including federal and state income tax as well as self-employment tax, can be more than 50% of the profit from exercising the stock option. Let me say even more strongly: *plan ahead.*

Selling the shares

When you sell your shares you'll report capital gain or loss, and that means you need to know your *holding period* and your *basis.*

Holding period. Your holding period is used to determine whether your gain or loss on the sale is short-term or long-term. The rule here is that your holding period begins when you acquire the shares—you don't get to count the time you held the option. Any gain or loss will be short-term if you sell within a year after exercising the option; long-term if you wait at least a year and a day.

Basis. Most of the time, when you buy and sell stock, your basis is the amount you paid for the shares (including brokerage commissions). Not here! When you exercise a nonqualified stock option, your basis is the amount you paid for the shares *increased by the amount of income you reported on exercising the option.* That's an important point, because it saves you from having to pay tax twice on the same profit. Let's look at our earlier example again.

> **Example:** You exercise a $12 option to buy 1,000 shares when the stock is trading at $18. After holding the shares for a while, you sell them at $22. You report $6,000 of compensation income on the exercise of the option and $4,000 of capital gain when you sell the shares.

You paid $12,000 when you exercised the option, and ended up selling the shares for $22,000. How did you get away with reporting only $4,000 of capital gain? Easy: your basis includes the $6,000 of compensation income you reported on exercising the option. On Form 8949 (the part of your tax return listing individual capital gains and losses), you'll report this sale the same as if you paid $18,000 for the shares.

You can see how a mistake here could be costly. If you report only the amount you actually paid for the shares, you would end up paying tax on $6,000 of compensation income and $10,000 of capital gain. That's a total of $16,000, even though your actual profit is only $10,000.

When you report a sale of the shares, be sure to increase your basis by the income from exercising the option.

Capital loss

You may end up selling your shares at a price lower than the value on the date of exercise. In that case you'll report a capital loss—even if you have an overall profit from your stock option.

> **Example:** You exercise a $12 option to buy 1,000 shares when the stock is trading at $18. After holding the shares for a while, you sell them at $14.

Selling the shares at a lower price doesn't change the amount of compensation income you have to report on the exercise of the option: it's still $6,000. When you report the sale of the stock, you'll show a $4,000 *capital loss*. The combination of these two numbers ($6,000 of income and $4,000 of capital loss) is equal to your actual profit of $2,000.

Here's the problem. There are lots of times when the added tax from the compensation income is bigger than the tax reduction from the capital loss.

- You pay social security tax or self-employment tax on the compensation income, but you don't get a break on those taxes when you have a capital loss.

- You may be forced to use your capital loss as an offset to long-term capital gain, which is taxed at lower rates than ordinary income.

- Most important of all, the $3,000 capital loss limitation can prevent you from using the entire loss in the year you sell the shares. Unused loss can be carried forward but not back.

When the numbers get big enough, the effect of the capital loss limitation can be devastating.

> **Example:** You pay $100,000 (plus withholding and social security tax) to exercise your nonqualified stock option when the stock is worth $600,000, financing the purchase with a margin loan so that you can hold the shares. Then everything starts to go wrong. The stock market heads

south, and your company does worse than most when it turns out that someone was cooking the books to make earnings look stronger than they really were. You hold on expecting a recovery but the bad news keeps on coming, and you end up selling the stock for $150,000.

Overall, you still have a profit of $50,000 (less expenses, such as margin interest). That's disappointing compared with the $500,000 you could have had if you sold the stock when you exercised the option, but at least it's something. Or is it? You have to report $500,000 of compensation income. You also have a capital loss of $450,000, but you get to use only a paltry $3,000 of that amount in the current year. Your total bill for federal and state income tax could be $200,000 or more. The law says you have to pay that tax, even if it's greater than the amount realized when you sold the stock.

You may be thinking a disaster like this can't happen to your company's stock. Yet nearly all stocks have suffered declines of more than 50% at one time or another, including many high quality, "blue chip" stocks. The capital loss limitation is an important fact of life when you plan to hold shares after exercising a nonqualified stock option.

Out of the frying pan. One guy I know exercised his options and sold the stock right away, but invested the money in a small number of technology stocks that performed like the proverbial lead balloon. The results were just as bad as if he held onto the option shares, leaving him with a tax bill that was greater than his profit. To protect against this risk you have to put at least some of your option profit into safer investments. The stock market can be a great place to invest, but there's always risk of a short-term loss, and that risk is intensified if you fail to diversify broadly.

> Any part of your option profit that's needed to pay taxes should be invested conservatively.

Same-day sales

Some people exercise their options and sell the stock all in one fell swoop. You might do this to turn the entire option profit into cash, or you might sell only some of the shares. One popular approach is called "sell to cover": you sell just enough shares to cover the cost of exercising the option, including withholding and employment tax.

A same-day sale doesn't necessarily eliminate capital gain or loss. Your actual sale proceeds depend on the trading price for the stock at the precise moment the sale occurs. The value used to determine your compensation income may be the *average* value for that day, or the previous day's closing value, which may be higher or lower than your sale proceeds. What's more, if you pay a brokerage commission on the sale, it reduces your sales proceeds but doesn't reduce the amount of compensation income you report.

The upshot is that even when you sell shares at the same time you exercise your option, you can end up having capital gain or loss on the sale. Usually the amount is too small to worry about, but if the stock price happens to move sharply on the date of exercise you can see a difference that makes a difference.

Double reporting, but no double tax

Exercising the option and selling the shares are two different things you have to report on your tax return, even if you do both simultaneously. You'll see the compensation income from exercising the option appear as part of your wages on Form W-2 if you're an employee, so there's nothing special you have to do there. Just report the full amount of wages as you always do. You also have to fill out Form 8949, used to report individual sales, and Schedule D, which aggregates capital gain and loss information from Form 8949 and other sources. Even if your gain or loss is zero, you have to report the sale.

No double tax. Chances are that you'll receive a report called Form 1099-B early in the year after you sell your shares. Some people are concerned the first time they see this form because it may seem to indicate that the gain is larger than it should be. Nowadays brokers are required to report basis on this form for certain stock transactions, but due to the way this law was implemented, it's possible that basis will be omitted when you sell your option stock, or it may be reported as the amount you paid for the shares even though your true basis includes the amount of income you reported for exercising the option. You aren't stuck with those numbers, however. If you receive a Form 1099-B that doesn't include basis, you'll indicate that fact on Form 8949 and show the correct basis. There's also a way to indicate on Form 8949 that basis reported by the broker has to be increased to reflect income reported on exercise of the option.

> Be sure to include the compensation income in your basis, as explained earlier in this chapter.

Special situations

There are other tax rules that can apply to special situations:

- "Early exercise plans" allow you to exercise options before the stock is vested. If your company has this type of plan, see Chapter 25.

- Some companies allow option holders to use shares of stock they already own to pay the exercise price. See Part VI for details.

Gifts of nonqualified stock options

Many nonqualified stock option plans prohibit transfers of options, except perhaps at death. Some companies make their nonqualified options transferable to a limited extent, usually only for estate planning purposes. What follows is a brief summary of some tricky rules, not a complete guide. Be sure to consult with an expert before using this strategy.

No income shift. Transferring a nonqualified stock option doesn't shift the income tax consequences of exercising the option. Even though you'll no longer own the option, you'll have to report income when the option is exercised, just as if you were the one to exercise it. The ability to transfer your option is not an opportunity for income tax planning.

Gift and estate tax. The potential benefit from transferring an option comes in connection with gift and estate tax. Even here, it isn't easy to achieve tax savings. The IRS requires you to use recognized procedures (such as the Black-Scholes formula) to determine the value of the stock option for gift tax purposes. The transfer can backfire if the value of the option goes down after you transfer it.

In addition, the IRS says you haven't made a completed gift if you transfer an option prior to vesting. The gift tax is triggered when the option vests, and by that time the value can be a lot higher. You might end up owing more income tax and gift tax than you anticipated, but you can't use the option profit to pay those taxes because you no longer own the option.

14

Nonqualified Options and Capital Gain

Here's a strategy that seems to make sense but doesn't really work.

SUPPOSE YOU HAVE A NONQUALIFIED OPTION that still has plenty of time to run. You're confident the stock price is going to rise, and it occurs to you that this increase in value will end up being taxed as compensation income when you exercise the option. That means paying the highest income tax rates. Wouldn't it be smarter to exercise the option *now* and hold onto the stock? That way the price increase you're expecting will produce a capital gain. If you hold the stock more than a year, you'll have *long-term* capital gain and pay federal tax at a reduced rate.

It turns out that if your company's stock is *publicly traded*—meaning you can buy and sell shares in the stock market—this strategy isn't so smart. Even when you have complete confidence the stock price will rise, you're better off continuing to hold the option. That seems like a strange conclusion, but it follows from some fairly simple logic explained below. We'll work from the assumption that you have an option to buy 1,000 shares at $10 per share. You plan to sell the stock when it reaches $110—an increase of $100 per share, or $100,000 overall—and expect that will happen by the time your option expires. To make things simple, we'll also assume any compensation income you receive is taxed at a combined state and federal rate of 40%, and capital gains are taxed at a combined state and federal rate of 20%. That means you end up with $60,000 after tax if you wait until the stock reaches $110 before exercising the option.

Zero spread exercise

One possible strategy is to exercise the option when there is no gain at all. You're hoping to capture *all* your profit as long-term capital gain by exercising when the market price of the stock is $10 per share. That's a high-risk choice because you lose money if the stock price drops at all, but we're assuming your confidence in the stock is strong enough to make you comfortable with that risk. If things go as planned the stock will rise to $110 while you hold it more than a year. When you sell it, your $100,000 profit will be long-term capital gain. You end up with $80,000 after paying the 20% state and federal capital gains tax. This strategy appears to be better than holding the option while the stock price climbs to $110: on an after-tax basis you end up with $20,000 more.

Yet there's a fatal flaw in this reasoning. You would be foolish to exercise the option when you can buy the stock in the market for the same price. Using $10,000 to buy stock in the market doesn't expose you to any greater risk than using the same amount to exercise the option. The profit is the same, too, and so is the tax. Buying the stock in the market puts you in the same position in every respect except one: you still have the option. So when the stock reaches $110, you sell the stock for a profit of $100,000 (taxed at 20%) *and* you cash out the option—exercise and sell the stock—for *another* $100,000 of profit. The second $100,000 is taxed as compensation at higher rates, of course, but you are *far* better off than if you exercised the option when the stock price was $10.

> For publicly traded stock, it doesn't make sense to exercise a nonqualified stock option that isn't in the money.

Midterm exercise

So far we've learned that it doesn't make sense to exercise the option at the very beginning of its journey from $10 to $110. What about exercising halfway through that journey, when the stock is at $60? That way you capture at least *some* of your profit as long-term capital gain, while avoiding the mistake of exercising the option when you could have bought the stock in the market for the same price.

What's wrong with this plan? When you exercise the option you have to come up with $30,000: $10,000 to pay the exercise price plus another $20,000 to pay the 40% state and federal tax on your $50,000 profit. Remember, with a nonqualified stock option you have to pay this tax even if you don't sell the stock. When you factor in the need for this $30,000, the "midterm exercise strategy" we're considering becomes unattractive.

Sell to cover. One way to come up with this money is to "sell to cover." At the time you exercise the option, you give instructions for the immediate sale of enough shares to pay the exercise price and the tax. We're doing all this when the stock is trading at $60, so you need to sell 500 shares—half your holdings—to come up with the $30,000. You hold the other 500 shares until the stock price reaches $110 and then sell. You receive $55,000 in the sale (500 shares times a value of $110) and pay $5,000 capital gains tax, leaving you with $50,000. (You had $25,000 of capital gain as the value of the stock rose from $30,000 to $55,000, so at 20% your tax is $5,000.) Remember, though, you would have had *$60,000* if you simply held the option until the stock price reached $110. Using a "sell to cover" approach to convert future appreciation to long-term capital gain is a losing proposition.

Using other funds. Perhaps you don't have to sell to cover. You're able to come up with $30,000 to exercise the option and pay the tax without selling any of the stock. Using this approach you'll end up selling 1,000 shares for a total of $110,000. You have to pay $10,000 capital gains tax on this sale, and you came up with $30,000 when you exercised the option, so your net with this approach is $70,000. That's $10,000 *more* than if you waited until the stock reached $110 to cash in your option.

The problem here is a variation on the problem with the zero spread exercise discussed earlier. The $30,000 you used to exercise the option would have produced a bigger profit if you used it to buy shares in the market. With that much money you could buy an additional 500 shares. When the stock reaches $110 you sell those shares for $55,000. After paying $5,000 capital gains tax you have a profit of $20,000. We saw earlier that you can gain $10,000 in after-tax profit by using your $30,000 to exercise the option. Using the $30,000 instead to buy stock gives you twice that benefit, a profit of $20,000.

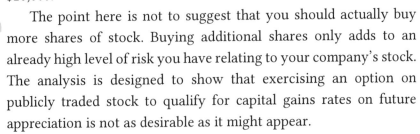

The point here is not to suggest that you should actually buy more shares of stock. Buying additional shares only adds to an already high level of risk you have relating to your company's stock. The analysis is designed to show that exercising an option on publicly traded stock to qualify for capital gains rates on future appreciation is not as desirable as it might appear.

The "midterm exercise strategy" does not maximize the after-tax profit from your stock option.

Conclusion

The surprising conclusion of all this analysis is that the best strategy in this situation is the one that ends up making you pay the most tax. The leverage provided by continuing to hold the option is more powerful than the benefit you can achieve by taking advantage of the lower tax rate for long-term capital gains. Here are some important limitations on this conclusion:

Option expiration. The analysis above assumes your option has plenty of time to run at the time you're planning your strategy. The decision process when the option is about to expire is different. In that situation you should exercise an option that's in the money and make a decision about whether to hold the shares based on investment considerations, focusing especially on investment risk as described in Chapter 5.

Incentive stock options. Incentive stock options provide added tax benefits that encourage you to hold the shares after exercising the option. For analysis, see Chapter 18.

Privately held companies. The arguments presented above rely heavily on your ability to buy stock in the market. That opportunity doesn't exist for companies that are not publicly traded. This is why many pre-IPO companies offer early exercise stock option plans, permitting option holders to exercise before the stock is vested. As discussed in Chapter 28, the strategy of exercising to hold pre-IPO stock is risky but potentially rewarding.

Part V
Incentive Stock Options and AMT

15

Regular Tax Rules for ISOs

Under the regular income tax, you pay no tax when you exercise an incentive stock option. If you hold the shares long enough, the profit becomes long-term capital gain.

ECONOMICALLY, INCENTIVE STOCK OPTIONS are just like nonqualified stock options. You can lay the two side by side and see no difference at all other than the fact that one is called an incentive stock option and the other is not. Yet the tax rules for ISOs are far more complex. Proper handling of them requires more knowledge, and more detailed planning, than are required for nonqualified options.

There's a reason to endure these headaches, though. Incentive stock options provide the possibility of paying significantly less tax than if you received nonqualified stock options. Both types of option can provide the same economic profit, but with an ISO you get to *keep* more of that profit.

The main benefit from having an incentive stock option instead of a nonqualified stock option is the opportunity to convert some or all of your profit into long-term capital gain, even though the profit built up while you were still holding the stock option. To obtain this benefit, you have to satisfy special rules that apply only to ISOs, as described in this chapter. Unfortunately, you also have to deal with another set of rules under the *alternative minimum tax* (or *AMT*). Those rules are complicated enough to require separate discussion, which comes later.

Exercising an ISO

By now you're aware that you have to report compensation income when you exercise a nonqualified stock option. That isn't true for incentive stock options. In fact, under the regular income tax rules, you don't report anything at all. We'll see later that you may have to pay alternative minimum tax when you exercise your ISO, but under the regular income tax you have nothing to report until you sell or otherwise dispose of the shares.

> You may have to report income in dispositions other than sales, including gifts or charitable donations.

Special holding period

Your tax consequences for a sale or other disposition depend in part on how long you hold the shares. You don't get to convert your profit into long-term capital gain unless you hold the stock until *both* of the following are true:

- It is more than one year after the date you exercised the option, *and*

- It is more than two years after the date the option was granted.

In most cases you aren't allowed to exercise your option in the first year after you receive it, and in that case you don't have to worry about the second requirement. If you wait at least a year after the option was granted before exercising it, and also hold the stock more than a year after you exercise, you'll automatically be holding until more than two years after the grant date. The requirement to hold until at least two years after the option was granted is only important when you're allowed to exercise the option less than a year after it was granted, and you choose to do so.

> **Example:** You exercise an ISO six months after it was granted. In this case it won't be good enough to hold the shares for a year. To satisfy the special holding period you have to hold the shares 18 months, to a date more than two years after the option was granted.

We're going to see that there are times when you shouldn't even try to satisfy the holding period requirement. Sometimes it's better to sell some or all of the shares, even though that means paying tax at a higher rate. Plenty of people have been burned holding onto ISO stock to meet this requirement when they should have sold at least some of the shares earlier.

Sale of mature shares

If you satisfy the special holding period described above, we say your shares are *mature*. For purposes of the regular income tax, selling mature ISO stock is just like selling stock you bought on the open market. Your basis is equal to the amount you paid for the stock, and your holding period began when you exercised the option. Normally this means you'll report profit as long-term capital gain, paying a lower rate than you would pay on compensation income.

> If your overall income exceeds a threshold amount your profit may incur Medicare tax in addition to capital gain tax. Chapter 34 discusses Medicare tax on investment income.

You can also use ISO stock to make gifts or charitable contributions. Often this isn't a great idea, even after you hold mature ISO shares, for reasons we'll explain when we talk about the AMT credit. Under the regular income tax, though, you're free to treat mature ISO shares like any other shares of stock.

Early (or disqualifying) dispositions

Things start to get complicated when you sell or otherwise dispose of shares before satisfying the special holding period. The tax law calls this a *disqualifying disposition.* We'll save some wear and tear by using the term *early disposition* to mean the same thing. Before we learn the consequences of an early disposition, let's look at different kinds of transfers. Some of them count as dispositions, but others do not.

Transfer to broker. Transferring stock certificates to a broker who will hold the stock in street name isn't a disposition. The same is true when you transfer shares from one broker to another, provided that you are the owner of both brokerage accounts.

Death of shareholder. A transfer that occurs as a result of your death is not a disposition for purposes of this rule. Your death during the special holding period will not trigger compensation income.

Transfer to spouse. A transfer of the stock to your spouse—or to a former spouse in connection with a divorce—is not a disqualifying disposition. Following such a transfer, the spouse receiving the stock is subject to the same rules as the one who transferred the stock. If you receive ISO shares from your spouse you should also obtain essential information for tax reporting:

- The date when the special holding period ends.

- The cost basis of the shares.

- The value of the shares on the date the option was exercised.

Gifts and donations. Transfers at death and gifts to your spouse are covered by the rules described above. All other gifts are dispositions. You'll have to report compensation income if you give your ISO stock to an individual or donate it to a charity before the end of the special holding period.

Trusts. A custodial account under the Uniform Transfers to Minors Act (or the Uniform Gifts to Minors Act) is *not* a trust. Transfers to such accounts are gifts, and count as dispositions.

A transfer of ISO stock to a *revocable* trust should not be treated as a disposition. You can terminate this kind of trust and take the stock and other property back whenever you want. For that reason, the tax law treats you as if you still own the stock after you transfer it to a revocable trust.

You've made a disposition, though, if you transfer the stock to an *irrevocable* trust. This type of trust doesn't let you take the stock back out. Generally you'll want to avoid making such a transfer during the special holding period, because it means having to report compensation income.

Short sales. In a short sale, you sell shares you borrowed from another investor instead of selling shares you own. The IRS has taken the position that a short sale of your company's stock while you hold ISO stock ("selling short against the box") is a disposition. They may apply this rule even if the "constructive sale rule" that applies to certain short sales doesn't apply.

Market options. Within limits, you can use options you buy in the stock market to protect your gains in ISO stock without causing a disqualifying disposition. For example, you may be able to buy a put option that protects you against a decline in the value of the stock. Some of the tax consequences of doing this are unfavorable, however, and many companies discourage or prohibit employees from trading in market options on their stock. See Chapter 32 for more on this subject.

Borrowing. Using the stock as collateral for a loan is *not* a disposition. For example, you can hold the stock in a margin account with your broker without triggering compensation income. Of course, you'll have a disposition if the stock is sold to meet your margin requirements, or is otherwise seized as collateral. See below for bankruptcy, however.

Bankruptcy. A special rule protects you from having a disqualifying disposition in bankruptcy. You don't have a disposition when the stock is transferred to a bankruptcy trustee, or when the trustee transfers it to a creditor in satisfaction of a liability.

Sale to an unrelated person

The most common type of early disposition is a sale to an unrelated person, usually accomplished by having a broker sell the shares in the stock market. Assuming you don't purchase replacement shares of the same stock within 30 days before or after this sale, here are the tax consequences:

- For a sale below the amount you paid for the shares, you don't report any compensation income. Your loss on this sale is reported as a capital loss.

- For a sale above the amount you paid for the shares but no higher than the value of the shares as of the date you exercised the option, report your profit on the sale as compensation income (not capital gain). You also need to report the sale on your tax return, but you have no gain or loss on the sale. That's because your basis includes the compensation income you reported, making your basis equal to the selling price.

- If you sell your shares at a price that's higher than the value of the shares as of the date you exercised the option, you report two different items. The bargain element when you exercised the option (the difference between the value of the shares as of that date and the amount you paid) is reported as compensation income. Any additional profit is reported as capital gain (which is normally short-term).

You'll report this income in the year of sale. For regular income tax purposes, you don't report anything in the year you exercise the option unless you dispose of the shares in the same year.

No withholding or social security tax. For a while there was some question about whether you have to pay employment tax on exercise of incentive stock options. It's now clear there will be no income tax withholding or other employment tax on this income, even if you sell the shares the same day you exercise the option. Overall that's a good thing, but it means you can have one heck of a big tax bill on April 15. You may also have to make estimated tax payments as described in Chapter 31.

> **Example:** You exercise an ISO and sell the shares the same day for a profit of $200,000. There's no withholding, even though this is compensation income and you're going to owe over $60,000 in income tax.

You'll be fine, of course, if you set aside enough money to pay the tax. If you spend it, or lose it in a risky investment, you'll wake up with a headache on April 15. The IRS will insist on payment even if your profit has disappeared.

> Make sure you set aside enough cash to cover your tax liability when you exercise an incentive stock option.

Other early dispositions

The discussion above applies to the most common type of early disposition: a sale to an unrelated person. There's an unfavorable rule that applies to other types of dispositions. It applies in any situation where the tax rules would prevent you from deducting a loss. It doesn't matter if you have an *actual* loss. Even if you have a gain, the rule applies if the disposition was one of the *types* of transactions where losses are not allowed. The problem transactions are (1) gifts, including charitable gifts, (2) sales to relatives, or to entities (like trusts or businesses) owned by you or your relatives, and (3) any sale where you purchase replacement shares within 30 days before or after the sale. (As explained in Chapter 6, the wash sale rule can prevent you from claiming a loss when you buy replacement shares during this period.) In any of these situations, the following rules apply:

- You have to report the full amount of the bargain element from when you exercised the option as compensation income. That's true even if the value of the stock has gone down since the date you exercised the ISO.

- If the transaction requires you to report gain (such as a sale to a related person other than your spouse), any gain that exceeds the amount of compensation income should be reported as capital gain (which may be long-term or short-term depending on how long you held the stock).

Example: You paid $10,000 to buy stock worth $110,000 when you exercised your incentive stock option. You held onto the shares, and unfortunately the stock tanked. In December of the same year, the shares are worth just $20,000. A normal sale of the stock would allow you to report only $10,000 of compensation income.

Instead, you donate the stock to your favorite charity. Because of the unfavorable rule described above, you have to report compensation income equal to the original spread: $100,000. You also get a deduction for your charitable contribution, but that's only $20,000, the current value of the stock. You end up paying regular income tax on $80,000.

That's a stunning result. You didn't take any profit at all from the transaction. In fact, you invested $10,000 of your hard-earned money when you exercised the option, and ended up giving the shares to a charity. Yet you end up owing tens of thousands of dollars in income tax. *Don't make this mistake!*

16

Overview of AMT

AMT recalculates your tax under an alternative set of rules to determine the minimum amount of tax you have to pay.

THE BASIC IDEA BEHIND THE ALTERNATIVE MINIMUM TAX is a good one: people with very high levels of income shouldn't be able to completely avoid paying income tax while the rest of us pony up each year. The AMT is a poor reflection of that idea, however. Many high-income individuals escape its reach—and every year it ensnares many people who were never intended to be affected.

Whatever its merits or demerits, the AMT is a potential problem you have to deal with if you receive incentive stock options because exercise of ISOs frequently brings AMT into play. And it isn't just a matter of paying tax when you exercise your ISOs. You also have to understand the consequences when you sell the stock you acquired by exercising the options.

How it works

The alternative minimum tax is an extra tax some people have to pay on top of the regular income tax. The name comes from the way the tax works. The AMT provides an *alternative* set of rules for calculating your income tax. In theory these rules determine a *minimum* amount of tax that someone with your income should be required to pay. If you're already paying at least that much because of the "regular" income tax, you don't have to pay AMT. But if your regular tax falls below this minimum, you have to make up the difference by paying alternative minimum tax. This diagram sums it up:

Basic Concept of AMT

Calculate regular income tax using the normal rules ⇨	Use an alternative set of rules to calculate tentative minimum tax (TMT)

Compare regular tax with TMT

If regular tax is bigger, pay this amount and ignore TMT ⇔	If TMT is bigger, pay regular tax plus AMT to make up the difference

---

Notice that we are not merely adding an extra tax that applies to special items. Instead, we're using an alternative set of rules to recalculate the tax on *all* your income. If you have a normal item of income like salary or a distribution from an IRA, that item goes into both calculations. The key is that some items get different treatment under the AMT, increasing or decreasing the tax calculated under those rules.

Q: How do I know if I have to worry about the AMT?

A: Unfortunately, there's no good answer to this common question—which is one of the big problems with the AMT.

You can have AMT liability because of one big item on your tax return, or because of a combination of many small items. Some things that can contribute to AMT liability are items that appear on many tax returns, such as a deduction for state and local tax or interest on a second mortgage, or even your personal and dependency exemptions. If you use computer software to prepare your tax return, the program should be able to do the AMT calculation. If you're preparing a return by hand, the only way to know for sure is to fill out Form 6251—a laborious process.

AMT calculation

To understand alternative minimum tax you need to see how it's calculated. Here's the big picture.

Compute an alternate tax. First, you figure the amount of tax you would owe under a different set of income tax rules. What's different about these rules? Broadly speaking, three things:

- Various tax benefits that are available under the regular income tax are reduced or eliminated.

- You get a special deduction called the *AMT exemption*, which is designed to prevent the AMT from applying to taxpayers with modest income. This deduction *phases out* when your income reaches higher levels, a fact that causes significant problems under the alternative minimum tax.

- You calculate the tax using AMT rates, which start at 26% and move to 28% at higher income levels. By comparison, the regular tax rates start at 10% and then move through a series of steps to a high of 39.6%.

The result of this calculation is the amount of income tax you would owe under the "alternative" system of tax.

Compare with the regular tax. Then you compare this tax with your regular income tax. If the regular income tax is *higher*, you don't owe any AMT. If the regular income tax is *lower*, the difference between the two taxes is the amount of AMT you have to pay.

> **Example 1:** Your regular income tax is $47,000. When you calculate your tax using the AMT rules, you come up with $39,000. That's lower than the regular tax, so you don't pay any AMT. You pay only the regular income tax of $47,000.

> **Example 2:** Your regular income tax is $47,000. When you calculate your tax using the AMT rules, you come up with $53,000. You have to pay $6,000 of AMT on top of $47,000 of regular income tax.

If you're paying attention, you've probably noticed that the total amount of tax you pay in Example 2 is equal to the tax calculated under the AMT: $53,000. But it's important to note that you actually pay $47,000 of regular tax plus $6,000 of AMT, not $53,000 of AMT. You'll see the significance of that observation when we look at the AMT credit.

AMT exemption. Our brief summary above mentions a special deduction called the AMT exemption. This is a sizeable deduction: up to $82,100 for married couples, or $52,800 for singles, as of 2014. It gets phased out, though, beginning when your income reaches a specified level ($156,500 for married couples, $117,300 for singles, as of 2014), with every $100 of income above that level eliminating $25 of this deduction.

That may sound like a technicality, but it's a significant fact of life for anyone dealing with AMT. When you add $100 of income, you also lose $25 of your exemption amount, so the taxable amount increases by $125. At a 28% rate, the tax on this amount is $35. That means the *real* rate of tax under the AMT can be as high as 35%.

Whenever you estimate AMT, keep in mind that the highest *real* rate of tax is 35%, not 28%.

Reporting and paying the tax. To calculate and report your AMT liability you need to fill out *Form 6251, Alternative Minimum Tax— Individuals.* The instructions for that form are very useful, particularly because the IRS discontinued the publication it used to put out on the AMT.

> You're required to take your AMT liability into account in determining how much estimated tax you pay. See Chapter 31 on estimated tax.

What causes AMT liability?

In this book we're interested in AMT mainly because it matters to people who exercise incentive stock options. Yet there are a number of other items that can cause you to pay AMT. Even if these other items aren't enough to cause you to pay AMT, they can affect the *amount* of AMT you'll pay when you exercise an ISO.

Two items are far more important than the others. The first affects just about everyone. Believe it or not, personal exemptions contribute to AMT liability. The exemptions you claim for yourself, your spouse and your dependents are not allowed when calculating alternative minimum tax. If you have a large number of exemptions, you may run into AMT liability even without taking any of the special tax breaks the AMT was originally designed to curtail.

> A taxpayer with a large number of exemptions challenged the AMT in court, saying Congress didn't intend for the tax to apply to someone in his situation. But the law is clear on this point, and the court ruled for the IRS.

If you itemize, there's a good chance you claim a deduction for state and local tax, including property tax and either income tax or sales tax. These deductions are not allowed under the AMT. If you live in a place where state and local taxes are high, you're more likely to pay AMT.

These two items—personal exemptions and the itemized deduction for state and local taxes—account for something like 90% of the alternative minimum tax collected by the IRS. There are numerous other items that can cause you to pay AMT, however. The list includes itemized deductions that are reduced or eliminated, cutbacks on certain business deductions that are sometimes used to shelter income, and a rule that makes some (but not all) interest on municipal bonds taxable under the AMT. No doubt about it: alternative minimum tax is a big, complicated mess.

Long-term capital gain. One other item deserves mention. Some people encounter AMT when they have a large, long-term capital gain. People find this puzzling because capital gain is taxed at the same rate under the AMT as under the regular income tax. The problem is that you can lose some or all of your AMT exemption amount when your income grows, even if the growth comes from capital gains. A smaller AMT exemption amount means higher AMT, even if capital gains are taxed at the same rate under both tax systems.

> **Example:** You have a long-term capital gain of $100,000, and your overall income for the year is in the range where the tax rate on this gain will be 15%, so you pay $15,000 under the regular income tax. You pay 15% under the AMT as well, but this gain reduces your AMT exemption amount by $25,000. That means $25,000 of income that was previously sheltered from AMT is now subject to the tax, for an additional tax hit of up to $7,000 (28% of $25,000).

AMT credit

Our overview of the AMT wouldn't be complete without at least passing mention of the AMT credit. We'll deal with this topic later.

I'll warn you now, though, that many people misunderstand this credit, and that includes plenty of financial advisors and tax professionals. If you end up paying AMT when you exercise an incentive stock option, be sure to read our explanation of the AMT credit.

17

AMT and ISOs

If you hold ISO shares after the end of the year, the AMT rules treat you as if you exercised a nonqualified stock option.

YOU'RE PROBABLY EXPECTING this chapter to be at least somewhat complicated. I'm afraid that's the case. I could have made it simpler by leaving out some of the details, but often it's precisely these details that cause people to make expensive mistakes. This chapter may give you a headache, but that's nothing compared with the one you might get if you *don't* read it.

It's easier to understand these rules if you start out with an overview:

- You can ignore AMT if you sell your shares the same year you exercise your option. We'll explore later why you may or may not want to do this.

- If you hold ISO shares after the end of the year you exercise the option, the AMT rules treat you as if you exercised a nonqualified stock option. In other words, under the AMT the bargain element of the option is taxed in the year of exercise. Unless the bargain element is quite small, you're likely to pay AMT on top of your regular income tax.

- The AMT credit can reduce the amount of tax you pay in subsequent years—especially, but not exclusively, the year you sell your ISO shares. You may be disappointed, though, if you assume you'll recover all your AMT. Some people end up with a large unrecovered AMT credit after they sell the stock.

As usual, we're assuming in this chapter that your shares are vested when you exercise your stock option.

Disposition by December 31

There's one easy way to prevent your incentive stock options from causing AMT liability: sell your shares in the same tax year you exercise the option. This may or may not be your best choice—we'll talk about strategies later—but at least it's simple. In fact, it's the *only* thing about AMT that's simple.

Selling the shares (or otherwise disposing of them) in the same year you exercise the option causes you to have exactly the same treatment under the AMT as you have under the regular income tax. If you end up with $75,000 of compensation income under the regular income tax, you also have $75,000 of compensation income under the AMT. The income is treated the same under both tax systems, so you aren't doing anything to make your AMT bigger than your regular income tax.

Just remember we're talking about the end of tax year, which is December 31 for nearly everyone. We aren't talking about the year that begins when you exercise your stock option. If you exercise your option on October 31, you have just two months to sell the shares if you want to eliminate AMT.

> Selling shares in the same calendar year you exercised the option eliminates AMT—but also eliminates the opportunity to convert the profit from your stock option into long-term capital gain.

Holding after the end of the year

If you hold your ISO stock after the end of the year of exercise, the AMT treatment is quite different from the regular income tax treatment. In fact, the AMT treats you the same as if you held nonqualified stock options. You'll have to report compensation income equal to the bargain element: the amount by which the fair market value of the stock was greater than the exercise price of the option on the date of exercise. But you report this income only for AMT purposes, on Form 6251. That's why incentive stock options can cause you to pay AMT.

> **Example:** Before you exercised your incentive stock option, your regular income tax calculation produced a tax of $12,000, and the tax calculated under the AMT was $10,000. You exercised an ISO with a bargain element of $75,000 and held the shares after the end of the year. Your regular income tax calculation isn't affected at all—it's still $12,000—but you've added $75,000 of income, and about $20,000 of tax, to your AMT calculation. So now the tax calculated under the AMT is $30,000. That's $18,000 more than the regular income tax, so you have to pay $18,000 AMT in addition to $12,000 of regular income tax.

> AMT is included when you determine how much estimated tax you have to pay. See Chapter 31.

AMT cushion. Notice that you end up paying $18,000, even though the tax on this amount is $20,000 under the AMT. That's because you had a $2,000 difference between regular income tax and AMT before you exercised the option. I call this the *AMT cushion.* The size of your AMT cushion depends on all the factors mentioned in the previous chapter—items like personal exemptions and itemized deductions. Depending on your overall tax situation, this number could be zero (you might already be paying AMT before you exercise your ISO) or it could be as high as several thousand dollars. That means you may be able to exercise at least part of your ISO without paying any AMT at all.

Don't confuse this amount that I call the AMT cushion with the AMT exemption, which we discussed in the previous chapter. The AMT exemption amount can be as high as $82,100 (married filing jointly in 2014), but a lot of that gets eaten up by personal exemptions and other items. You might find that your AMT cushion is only around $2,000, as in the example above, even though your AMT exemption amount is much higher.

Take a deep breath

There's a lot more to the AMT story, but let's pause here for a moment. You may be wondering why anyone would bother holding onto ISO shares if they're going to pay all that AMT. The answer some people give is that you'll get the AMT back when you sell the shares. *That's wrong!* You may be able to claim AMT credit in a later year, but we're going to see that it won't necessarily be as much as the amount of AMT you paid in the year you exercised the option. For the most part, the AMT credit is a way of avoiding *additional* tax when you sell the shares, rather than a way of recovering the tax you paid in the year you exercised the option.

Yet in many cases there's still a good reason to hold at least some of the stock when you exercise an incentive stock option. The overall tax can be smaller—sometimes a lot smaller—even if you pay AMT when you exercise your option. In our most recent example, you paid $18,000 of AMT when you exercised an ISO with a bargain element of $75,000. You could have avoided AMT by selling the shares right away, but then you would have paid *regular* income tax on $75,000 of compensation income, at a tax cost that might be $25,000 or more. You would have liked to pay no tax at all, of course, but you might come out better paying $18,000 in AMT instead of $25,000 in regular income tax.

This points up one of the most common mistakes people make in thinking about incentive stock options. They think they've done something wrong if they ended up paying AMT, because it's an "added" tax on top of the regular income tax. In reality, paying AMT can be a way to reduce your overall tax bill. We'll return to that thought in the next chapter.

Dual basis and adjusted gain or loss

Ready to move on? When last seen, you were holding ISO shares you acquired in the previous year. What happens next is a little complicated but perfectly logical. Recall that for purposes of the AMT we're treating your option as if it were a nonqualified stock option. We're going to *continue* that treatment when you sell the shares.

Under the regular income tax, you didn't report any income for exercising the option, so your basis for the shares is simply the amount you paid. Under the AMT, though, you reported compensation income, and that amount is added to your basis for the shares. Your shares have dual basis: one number for regular tax, and a different number for AMT. When you sell them, the amount of gain or loss you have on a sale of the shares will be different under the AMT than it is under the regular income tax. The same transaction produces two different results!

Example: You pay $25,000 to exercise an ISO, buying shares worth $100,000 on the date of exercise. You hold onto the shares and report $75,000 under the AMT in the year of exercise. In a later year, after satisfying the special holding period, you sell the shares for $110,000.

Under the regular income tax, your basis for the shares is just $25,000, the amount you paid to exercise the option. You'll report a long-term capital gain of $85,000 ($110,000 sales proceeds minus $25,000 basis). Under the AMT, your basis for the shares is $100,000 because it includes the income you reported in the year of exercise. You'll report a long-term gain of just $10,000 under the AMT.

What's going on. Exercising your option boosted your AMT calculation above the regular income tax calculation in the first year. Selling the shares in a later year can produce a *lower* tax under the AMT, because you have a smaller gain on the sale. We'll return to this calculation shortly, but first, here's the moment you've been waiting for: let's meet the AMT credit.

AMT credit

The AMT credit is designed to prevent you from getting stuck paying tax on the same income twice, when the income is taxed under the AMT in one year and taxed under the regular income tax in a later year. The credit is *created* in a year you pay AMT, but *used* in a later year when you *don't* pay AMT. The credit doesn't reduce your AMT. It's called the AMT credit because it arises from paying alternative minimum tax in a prior year.

You need to have a *timing item* to create the AMT credit. A timing item is something that's taxed in one year under the AMT and in a later year under the regular income tax. Incentive stock options can create a timing item because AMT applies in the year of exercise, but the regular income tax doesn't apply until you sell the stock. If you pay AMT because of something that's not a timing item, such as a large number of personal exemptions, you don't create a credit.

Although you need a timing item to *create* the AMT credit, you don't need a timing item to *use* the credit. You can create the credit by exercising an incentive stock option, and use some or all of the credit in a later year even though you didn't sell any ISO stock that year. Many people assume they can't claim any AMT credit until they sell the shares, but that's wrong.

> **Example:** You exercise an incentive stock option and hold the shares, paying $3,000 in AMT. The next year you decide to continue holding the shares. Even though you didn't sell any stock, you may be able to claim some or all of the credit.

To claim the credit you have to file Form 8801. In fact, beginning with the year after you pay AMT, you have to file this form every year even if you *aren't* claiming any credit. That's how you get the unused credit to carry over to the next year. Once you've created this credit by paying AMT, you need to file Form 8801 every year until you've exhausted the credit by claiming the full amount.

It's safe to say that thousands of taxpayers overpay their taxes every year because of failure to file this form. If you use a computer to prepare your return, don't assume the software is smart enough to know you need this form, even if it "knows" you paid AMT in a previous year. Experience tells me the same is true even if you hire a professional to prepare your tax return. Failure to file this form can be an expensive mistake (though you may be able to correct it by filing an amended return within three years of the original due date). *Don't forget Form 8801.*

If you've created an AMT credit by exercising an incentive stock option, you need to file Form 8801 in every subsequent year until the credit is used up.

The credit as an asset

A great deal of misunderstanding (and bad tax planning) arises from thinking of the AMT credit as a way to recover tax you paid in the year you had AMT liability. That's true in a sense, but thinking of the credit that way is likely to lead to confusion. Instead, think of it as a way to reduce the tax you pay on income received in later years.

Why is that important? Many people are unhappy with having an unused AMT credit because they think this means the government is holding money they should be able to get back. To "recover" the credit they take steps like selling ISO stock or accelerating other income. They feel better when they've used more of the credit, and best of all when they've used it all.

In reality, having an unused AMT credit is a good thing. It's an asset that can be used to reduce your income tax in future years. Much of the planning designed to "make full use" of the credit needlessly burns up the credit without producing any compensating advantage. Professional planners sometimes go to great lengths to work out arrangements allowing their clients to avoid having unused AMT credit—by volunteering to pay more tax than necessary.

Use the AMT credit to reduce taxes. Don't use taxes to reduce the AMT credit.

Calculating the credit

Working with the AMT credit is a two-step process. First you find out how much credit is *available*, then you find out how much of the available credit you can *use*.

Find the available credit. The first part of your task is to find out how much of the AMT liability from a *prior* year is *eligible* for the credit. This involves recalculating the alternative minimum tax under a special set of rules—sort of an *alternative* AMT. What you're doing here is finding out how much of your alternative minimum tax liability came from *timing* items: items that allow you to *delay* reporting income, as opposed to items that actually *reduce* the amount of income or tax you report. If you're lucky, your entire AMT will be available as a credit in future years. But some people find that only a portion, or none at all, is available for use as a credit. Fortunately, the adjustment for exercise of an incentive stock option is considered a timing item, so any AMT you pay because of exercising an ISO is eligible for the AMT credit.

Part I of Form 8801 is designed to determine how much AMT credit you have available.

Determine how much AMT credit you can use. If you have some AMT credit available from a prior year, you have to determine how much of the credit you can use in the current year. You can only use the AMT credit in a year when you're *not* paying alternative minimum tax.

The amount of AMT credit you can use is based on the difference between your regular tax and the tax calculated under the AMT rules.

> **Example:** Suppose you have $8,000 of AMT credit available from last year. This year your regular tax is $37,000, and your tax calculated under the AMT rules is $32,000. You don't have to pay AMT because your regular tax is higher than the tax calculated under the AMT rules. Better still, you're allowed to claim $5,000 of AMT credit, reducing your regular tax to $32,000. You can't use the credit to reduce your regular tax below the AMT for the year, though.

In this example, you would still have $3,000 of AMT credit you haven't used. That amount will be available next year. In tax lingo, it's *carried forward.*

Of course, you can't claim more than the amount of the available credit. In the example, if the AMT credit available from last year was $2,700, then you would use the full amount of the credit this year. You would reduce your regular tax to $34,300—*not* all the way to $32,000.

Part II of Form 8801 is designed to determine how much of your available AMT credit you can use.

Now that you see how the AMT credit works you can appreciate the significance of the adjustment you get when you sell ISO shares. It's a favorable adjustment—one that makes your tax *smaller* under the AMT—and that can help you claim a bigger AMT credit.

> **Example:** You paid AMT of $10,000 in the year you exercised your ISO and held the shares. A year later, you calculate that you can recover $2,000 of AMT credit without selling the shares. If you sell them, you'll report $40,000 of long-term capital gain under the regular income tax. Assuming this gain falls in the bracket where capital gain is taxed at 15%, your regular income tax on this gain would be $6,000. Under the AMT you have only $10,000 of capital gain for a tax of $1,500. (That's because the shares went up in value by $10,000 after you exercised the option.) The sale increases the gap between your regular income tax and the amount calculated under the AMT, so you claim an additional $4,500 in AMT credit.

In this example, you claimed a total AMT credit of $6,500 in the year you sold the shares. Without the favorable adjustment from selling the shares, you would claim only $2,000 of AMT credit.

> **Note:** This example illustrates the point made in the previous section. Selling these shares allowed you to use $4,500 of your AMT credit, but did not reduce your overall tax by $4,500. In fact, your overall tax increased by $1,500.

The effect of the credit was to reduce the amount of tax you paid on selling the shares, not to provide a refund of the AMT you paid previously.

More about selling ISO shares

I know you'll hate me for saying this, but things are more complicated than we've seen so far. That's because the AMT requires you to do a separate calculation of capital gains and losses. In this calculation, you combine the gain or loss you have from selling your ISO shares with any other capital gain or loss you have in the same year. According to the IRS, you have to fill out two versions of Schedule D (the form used for capital gains and losses): one for the regular income tax (which you file with your tax return) and a separate one for the AMT calculation (which you don't file, but retain for your records).

This isn't just a paperwork burden. It's a rule that can cost you a lot of money, by reducing the amount of AMT credit you claim. That's mainly because of the $3,000 capital loss limitation. Remember that rule? The amount of capital loss you deduct in any year is limited to the amount of capital gain you have in that year plus $3,000. If you have an overall capital loss of $60,000, you deduct $3,000 and carry over $57,000 to the next year. *The IRS says you have to apply this limitation separately in the AMT calculation.*

> **Example:** You pay $25,000 to exercise an ISO, buying shares worth $100,000 on the date of exercise. You hold onto the shares and report $75,000 under the AMT in the year of exercise. In a later year, after satisfying the special holding period, you sell the shares for $40,000.

Oops, your shares went *down* in value after you exercised the option. You still have a profit of $15,000, and you report that profit as a long-term capital gain under the regular income tax. Under the AMT, your shares have a basis of $100,000, so you report a capital *loss* of

$60,000. If this is the only item of capital gain or loss on your tax return, you'll claim $3,000 of this *AMT capital loss* in the year you sold the shares, and carry the rest over to the next year.

Here's why that's important. In the year you exercised your option, you added $75,000 to your AMT income. In the year you sold the stock, you subtracted only $18,000 from your AMT income. You get to eliminate the $15,000 *gain* that appears on your regular Schedule D, and deduct the $3,000 *loss* that appears on your AMT Schedule D. Add them together, and you get an adjustment of $18,000. The other $57,000 hangs around for possible use in future years, always subject to the limit of net capital gain plus $3,000 per year.

In effect, you're stuck with phantom income under the AMT. If that seems unfair, keep in mind that this is exactly what happens under the *regular* income tax if you exercise a *nonqualified* stock option. You would report $75,000 of income when you exercise the option, and you would be limited to a $3,000 capital loss when you sell the shares. If there's a problem here, it's a problem with the capital loss limitation—not a problem with the AMT.

Combining other capital gains and losses. If you have capital gains and losses from other sources, you have to combine them with your capital gain or loss from the ISO shares. The results can be interesting.

> **Example:** Same as the previous example (an AMT capital loss of $60,000 on selling your ISO shares), except this time you happen to have an unrelated capital gain of $80,000 from cashing in a mutual fund investment.

In this case you'll get to use the entire $60,000 capital loss, because the $3,000 capital loss limitation doesn't take effect until after you offset all your capital gains. It doesn't matter that the capital gain came from an unrelated item that doesn't get any special treatment under the AMT.

How the AMT credit plays out

How will the AMT credit play out on your tax return? The answer depends on your individual circumstances. The following observations that may help you know what to expect.

To begin with, in normal years many people have at least a small AMT cushion (difference between the tax calculated under the regular income tax rules and the tax calculated under the AMT rules). The size of that cushion depends on many factors, including the number of exemptions on your tax return and the amount of state and local tax you claim as an itemized deduction. This cushion can make it possible to use some or all of the AMT credit from exercising ISOs without selling the ISO stock.

> **Example:** Suppose you normally have an AMT cushion of about $2,000. In the first year you exercise enough ISOs to incur $3,000 of alternative minimum tax, and this entire amount is eligible for the AMT credit. In the following year you don't have any AMT adjustments: you didn't sell your ISO stock, and you didn't exercise any more ISOs either. In other words, this is a "normal" year for you. In that case, you should be able to claim about $2,000 of your AMT credit, because of your AMT cushion. You would have another $1,000 of AMT credit you didn't use, and that would carry forward to the next year.

Selling some or all of the ISO stock will usually produce a *favorable* AMT adjustment and increase the amount of credit you can claim. If we change the example above so that you sell enough ISO stock in the second year to create a favorable adjustment of $4,000, the AMT cushion would grow to more than $3,000 and you would be able to use the entire credit that year.

Unused credit. You can end up with unused AMT credit even after selling all your ISO stock. This can happen because your favorable adjustment upon sale of the stock is smaller than the adjustment that caused you to pay AMT in the year you exercised the option. As explained earlier, you can end up with a smaller adjustment because of the AMT capital loss limitation.

Example: You use an incentive stock option to buy stock worth $100,000 for $18,000. You pay $20,000 of AMT, creating an available credit in that amount for future years. The stock price collapses, and the following year you sell the stock for $30,000, with no other capital gains or losses. Because of the AMT capital loss limitation, your favorable adjustment is only $15,000 (the difference between the $12,000 gain under the regular income tax and the $3,000 loss allowed under the AMT). As a result you recover only a fraction of the $20,000 available AMT credit.

You can also have unused AMT credit because of a mismatch in tax rates: you pay AMT at 26% or 28% (or up to 35% when the AMT exemption amount is being phased out), but claim the credit against income that's taxed as long-term capital gain at lower rates. This is usually a significant issue only for people with very valuable incentive stock options.

Example: You exercise ISOs when the spread is $1,000,000. Your AMT liability from this transaction is about $280,000. The next year, after you satisfied the special holding period for ISO stock, you sell the stock for a price equal to the value of the stock when you exercised the option. For regular tax purposes you report a long-term capital gain of $1,000,000 and pay $200,000 on that gain (your income including this gain is high enough to make the 20% capital gain rate apply). You get to eliminate the entire $1,000,000 gain when you calculate your tax under the AMT, but that allows you to claim only about $200,000 of the AMT credit, because that's how much regular income tax you paid on that gain. A large portion of your credit remains unused.

The remaining credit will carry forward to future years. Perhaps you'll be able to use it in dribs and drabs over a number of years. When the dollar amounts are large enough, though, it's possible that you'll never recover the full value of the credit.

Comment. Now you see why the AMT credit isn't necessarily a way to recover the AMT you paid in the year you exercised your incentive stock option. Some option holders recover the entire credit, but many do not. In many cases it's more accurate to think of the credit as a way of protecting you from paying a second layer of tax on the same income that was already taxed under the AMT.

Refundable AMT credit

A more generous version of the AMT credit was available for a number of years, but 2012 was the last year it was allowed. What's more, this *refundable AMT credit* was allowed only for AMT credit that remained unrecovered more than three years, and that means it wasn't available for AMT incurred after 2008. This temporary measure was designed as a relief provision for people caught up in the AMT tsunami that engulfed thousands when the tech stock bubble of the late 1990s burst in the early 2000s. Because this version of the AMT credit has expired, it is now possible for AMT credit to remain unused for an indefinite number of years.

State AMT

Some states (notably California, home of many companies that provide incentive stock options) have their own version of the alternative minimum tax. When you figure the cost of exercising your ISOs, don't forget the possibility of paying state AMT.

There's potential for a double whammy here. State income tax (including state AMT) is a deduction on your federal return if you itemize. But the deduction isn't allowed when you calculate your federal AMT. Paying state AMT can increase your federal AMT!

18

Exercising ISOs to Hold the Stock

Up to a point, holding shares from an incentive stock option can provide a handsome benefit even if you pay AMT, but holding too many shares can expose you to risk and even increase your overall tax cost.

ISOS PROVIDE A SPECIAL BENEFIT if you hold the stock after exercising the option. Under the regular income tax you don't have to report income until you sell or otherwise dispose of the stock, and if you hold the stock long enough your profit on sale of the stock will be long-term capital gain. These benefits are offset by the requirement to pay AMT in the year of exercise and the risk of holding a concentrated stock position for at least a year. Beginning in 2013, you also face the possibility of paying Medicare tax on the capital gain you report when selling the stock. In this chapter we look at the economics of holding ISO stock. Is it worth it?

It depends

You knew I was going to say that, right? The answer depends on where the balance tips between the tax benefit you can expect to obtain if you hold the shares, and the diversification benefit (and sometimes tax savings) you get from selling the shares right away. There isn't any formula that allows a direct comparison between the two, but we can gain some insight into the tax benefit and then draw some general conclusions.

Three big factors

There are three big factors that determine how much tax benefit you get from holding the shares. One is your tax bracket, the second is a number I call the *profit percentage* of your stock option, and the third is the AMT impact.

Tax bracket. The benefit of holding ISO shares comes from converting ordinary income to long-term capital gain. That means your potential benefit differs according to your tax bracket. In the 25% tax bracket, you're reducing your tax by 10 percentage points when you qualify for the 15% capital gains rate. In the 35% tax bracket you save twice as much, reducing your tax by 20 percentage points. It can be worthwhile to hold ISO shares when you're in the 25% or 28% brackets, but the benefit is greater when you move up the ladder.

Bear in mind that your normal tax bracket won't necessarily apply to all your option income. If you exercise an option with a large bargain element, the income can push you into a higher tax bracket.

Profit percentage. An even more important factor in determining whether to hold shares is something I call the *profit percentage* of your stock option. This is the bargain element of the option divided by the total value of the shares at the time you exercise it. For example, if your option allows you to buy $100,000 worth of stock for $15,000, the profit percentage is 85% (bargain element of $85,000 divided by $100,000 share value). When the profit percentage is high, the benefit of holding the shares is greater because you don't have a lot of money tied up in the stock. When the profit percentage is low, you get less bang for your buck (and have more risk of loss) when you hold the shares because you have more money invested.

AMT impact. The third big factor determining the tax benefit from holding the shares is the AMT impact. This varies depending on which of the following categories apply to you:

- You can exercise the option and hold the shares without paying any AMT at all.

- You'll pay AMT if you hold the shares, but you can expect to make full use of the AMT credit.

- You'll end up with more AMT credit than you can expect to use.

Exercising without AMT

Unless you're already paying AMT for some reason, you can probably exercise at least some ISOs without paying AMT. If you're like most people, the amount of bargain element you can harvest this way is probably no more than $5,000 or $10,000. Whatever the number may be, you can reap a better tax benefit from those shares than you'll get if you have to pay AMT.

That doesn't necessarily mean you want to hold all the shares you can without paying AMT. If the profit percentage for your option is on the low side, you might be taking too much risk for the amount of tax benefit you can expect. Yet if your profit percentage is high, these are the shares that give you the greatest tax advantage.

Example: You're in the 28% tax bracket and have an option that allows you to buy $10,000 worth of shares for $2,000. Running a tax projection, you find that you can hold the shares without paying AMT.

Holding the shares ties up the $2,000 you used to exercise the option and exposes you to the risk that some or all of your $8,000 profit will disappear. Yet it also will allow you to reduce your tax rate on the profit from 28% to 15%. Because the profit percentage of the option is so high (80%), the tax benefit translates into a healthy boost in your expected return from holding this investment for one year. That means this could be a risk worth taking, if your overall financial situation is such that you can afford to maintain this much of an investment in your company's stock.

AMT credit recovered

Many people find themselves in a situation where they have to pay AMT in the year they exercise an ISO, but can reasonably expect to recover the full amount of the tax as an AMT credit when they sell the shares a year later. When that happens, the total amount of tax you save by holding shares is the same as if you never paid AMT in the first place. Yet you incurred more risk, and also got a somewhat diluted benefit because you had to pay the tax one year and recover the credit the next year. These factors reduce the overall benefit, but holding the shares can still make sense when the profit percentage is high, especially if you're in a high tax bracket. In marginal cases the reduced benefit may lead you to sell immediately after exercising the option.

Unrecovered credit

You may find that you aren't able to recover all your AMT as a credit, especially if your ISO has a large bargain element.

Example: You were in the right place at the right time and now find yourself ready to exercise an ISO that has a bargain element of $4,000,000. Your other income is small by comparison.

If you hold all the shares, your AMT for the year of exercise will be about $1,120,000. When you cash in that profit a year later (assuming the shares haven't lost value) the amount of AMT credit you'll claim will be about the same as the capital gains tax on that amount. At this level you'd be paying the highest capital gains rate of 20%, so you would use about $800,000 of the credit. Your unused AMT credit of about $320,000 carries over to future years but may end up being of little or no value.

Holding all the shares in a case like this is not likely to be the best strategy. You can sell some of your shares—perhaps a large portion—immediately after exercising the option without giving up any tax benefit. In fact, it's now possible to pay *less* tax by making a disqualifying disposition of some of your shares. We discuss this possibility under the heading "AMT Credit Balancing" in the next chapter.

ISO tax benefits in perspective

As always, you have to evaluate these tax benefits in the context of the amount of risk it is appropriate for you to take. Just because you can get a tax benefit from holding shares doesn't mean that's the right choice for you. It might make sense, in light of your financial condition and personal preferences, to hold fewer shares or none at all after exercising an incentive stock option.

On balance, though, in many situations it's reasonable to hold at least some of the shares. The tax benefit can boost the one-year return of the shares by 20% or more, so that if the stock goes up 10% you get an after-tax return equivalent to an investment that went up 30%—and you can come out ahead even if the stock price goes down, provided it doesn't fall too far.

19

ISO Strategies: Good, Bad and Ugly

Some ISO strategies save you money, but others merely sound good, and can cost more than they save.

IF YOU PLAN TO HOLD SOME OR ALL of the shares after exercising an incentive stock option, you should consider the strategies discussed below.

Exercise early in the year

One of the key pieces of advice to people exercising incentive stock options: *exercise early in the year.* There are two ways this can help you.

First, if you've held the option at least a year before exercising it, then you'll have to hold the stock only a year and a day before it's mature. If you exercised early in the year, you can sell before the following April 15 and use the sale proceeds to pay the AMT you owe as a result of exercising the option. That means you won't have to come up with cash out of pocket (or sell stock in a disqualifying disposition) to pay the tax.

Second, and often more important, exercising early in the year gives you the longest possible lookback period for the bail-out strategy discussed next.

Bailing out

In the year 2000, many people who followed the standard advice to exercise their incentive stock options early in the year found to their woe that they exercised just when the stock market (especially the market for tech stocks) was about to collapse. Some of those who continued to hold shares beyond the end of the year ended up with AMT liability greater than the remaining value of their shares. Many others escaped the potential tax trap, though, by selling the shares before the end of the year.

> **Example:** You exercised an incentive stock option with $1,000,000 of profit early in the year. It turned out to be a disastrous year for your company, and toward the end of the year the stock is worth $200,000. If you continue to hold the stock, you'll owe $280,000 in AMT—more than the value of your stock. If you sell before the end of the year, you still have sales proceeds of $200,000 and your taxable income is limited to your actual profit (if any). Bailing out reduces your taxes by over $200,000.

Your situation doesn't have to be that extreme for a bail-out to make sense. Any time the stock value has declined enough so that the regular tax you'll pay on a current sale is less than the AMT you'll owe if you continue to hold the shares, you should consider selling at least some of them as a hedge against a further decline in value.

Example: You paid $20,000 to exercise an incentive stock option for $100,000 worth of stock. Later that year the stock is worth $70,000. If you continue to hold the stock, your AMT will be $25,000. (This is more than 28% because some of the income fell in the range where your AMT exemption amount is phased out.) If you sell the stock now, you'll pay less than $18,000 in regular income tax. There's limited tax advantage in continuing to hold the stock, and risk that you'll find trouble if the stock declines further after the end of the year and before you can sell it. You should seriously consider selling at least some of the stock now to moderate your risk.

When planning for the possibility of bailing out, keep in mind the possibility that you'll be unable to sell shares during some periods. If you're subject to rules that prevent you from selling around the time the company issues its financial reports, be sure to know those rules. Likewise, consider any lockup period or Rule 144 restriction that might prevent you from selling shares. Leave a margin for error, because it isn't always possible to sell shares on the date you're planning a sale.

Bad bail-outs

Many realize they need to do something about their AMT problem when their shares decline in value but don't know what action to take. As indicated above, simply selling your stock through a broker will do the trick (assuming that alternative is available). Here are some things that *don't* work:

- **Giving your stock to a family member.** This is a disqualifying disposition, but because it is not a sale, you're required to report as ordinary income (compensation) the entire spread as of the date you exercised the option, not the smaller profit that existed as of the time of the gift. Actually, it doesn't matter whether your donee is a family member: any gift creates this problem.

- **Giving the stock to charity.** It may seem as if this should bail you out of your bad situation, but it can actually make matters worse. Once again you have a disqualifying disposition and you have to report the original option spread as compensation income. You also get a charitable contribution deduction, but this deduction is limited to the current value of the stock. See the example at the end of Chapter 15.

- **Selling your stock to a family member.** If you can't give the stock away, can you sell it to a family member? Sure, if you don't mind paying higher taxes. Once again, you're required to report the full spread from the time you exercised the option as compensation income.

- **Selling the stock and buying it back.** The rule here is the same as selling to a relative: if you buy the stock back within the "wash sale period" (which extends 30 days before and after the date of sale), you have to report the full spread from the date of exercise as compensation income. That's true even if you don't have a loss on the sale (the normal situation where the wash sale rule applies). A special rule says you're stuck paying the extra tax if your transaction even looks like a wash sale. Buying the stock back is likely to be a bad idea in any event—it's usually better to diversify—but if you feel this is the way you want to go, make sure you wait at least 31 days after your sale before buying replacement shares.

Year-end mini-exercise

If you're near the end of the year and thinking of exercising incentive stock options early the next year, consider exercising at least a small portion of your options before the end of the current year. The reason? In many situations you can exercise at least some options without incurring AMT. How much you can exercise with zero AMT depends on your situation. It can range from zero to tens of thousands of dollars. You'll have to do a calculation based on projected income and deduction figures to learn how big a freebie you can grab.

Eliminating AMT

Here's an idea that seems to make sense to lots of people, including some professional planners, but may not stand up to close scrutiny. You can eliminate AMT altogether on your incentive stock options if you use the "sell strategy" for some options and the "hold strategy" for others. If you work the numbers right, you won't pay any additional tax in the year you exercised your incentive stock options. Yet there's a hidden cost to this strategy.

> **Example:** Your income for the current year is $75,000 and your tax would be $14,500 if you didn't exercise any options. You decide to exercise incentive stock options that have a bargain element of $100,000. If you choose to hold all the shares until the end of the year, you'll owe $25,500 in AMT for total federal tax of $40,000. Spending some time with a calculator, you find that you can pay the same tax if you sell shares with $83,000 of profit and hold shares with $17,000 of profit. Your tax isn't any higher or lower, but now you're paying $40,000 of regular income tax and no AMT.

To many people this looks like a great idea. You avoided AMT, and you didn't pay any additional tax. The trouble is, you *will* pay additional tax the *following* year.

Here's why. If you held additional shares, incurring some AMT in the year you exercised the option, you would qualify for an AMT credit in the year of sale. When you sell enough shares to eliminate AMT completely, you eliminate the AMT credit as well. You have to look ahead to your likely tax situation in the year *after* you exercise an incentive stock option to get the complete picture of how these transactions will affect your taxes.

It can certainly make sense to sell shares to *reduce* the amount of AMT you pay in the year of exercise. That's a good way to moderate the amount of risk you bear from holding shares in your company's stock. What's more, as the previous chapter discusses, after a certain point your only benefit from holding additional shares is building up an unused AMT credit.

Selling enough shares to completely eliminate AMT in the year of exercise can reduce your overall tax benefit, though. It may be hard to imagine that you can actually get a better tax result by paying more AMT, but that's how it works.

AMT credit balancing

In some situations, especially when you have extremely valuable stock options, you may be able to project that you will end up with unused AMT credit after you sell your stock. A more sophisticated (and less costly) version of the strategy discussed above would be to sell just enough shares to eliminate the *excess* AMT credit: the credit that would otherwise be unused. I call this approach *AMT credit balancing*. It has several advantages:

- You obtain the maximum tax advantage available from converting ordinary income to capital gain.

- If your income (including option income and gain) is high, you avoid paying Medicare tax on capital gain that produced no tax benefit.

- Your sale of a portion of the shares provides cash with which to pay any tax you owe as a result of exercising the option.

- Any sale proceeds not used to pay tax can be used to diversify your investments.

Maximum tax advantage. The underlying assumption of the AMT credit balancing approach is that you will hold just enough shares to pay the amount of AMT that you can anticipate using later as a credit. When you do this, the total amount of tax paid, taking into account what you paid in the year you exercised the option and the year you sold the stock, including the effect of the AMT credit, is as low as possible. Holding additional shares will convert a greater amount of ordinary income into long-term capital gain, but the AMT deprives you of the potential tax benefit of this increment.

Avoiding Medicare tax. Beginning in 2013, high-income individuals pay a 3.8% tax on net investment income above certain levels (see Chapter 34). As of this writing, final regulations on this tax have not been issued. It appears, however, that it won't apply to ISO profit that's treated as compensation income. ISO profit is subject to this tax only to the extent it's converted to capital gain.

As a result, this tax reduces the benefit of converting ordinary income to capital gain. Conversion still produces a net benefit—until you reach the AMT credit balancing point. After that, you're no longer getting any benefit from conversion, so the only tax effect of holding more shares is to incur more Medicare tax. This means that under current law, *holding more shares can increase your total tax.* To put it another way, if you're subject to this tax, you can actually end up paying less tax by making a disqualifying disposition.

Cash for tax. Selling some of your shares right away after exercising an ISO will let you set cash aside for the tax you're going to owe—or perhaps send it in right away as an estimated tax payment. This is an important strategic advantage. You may feel there is little or no risk that you'll be unable to pay that tax through a later sale of shares, but there are plenty of people who had the same thought and ended up with a tax bill that exceeded the value of their shares. This is a side benefit, and an important one, of selling shares for AMT credit balancing. Make sure any money you're holding for later payment of tax is in a no-risk investment such as a certificate of deposit or money market fund.

Diversifying. Chapter 5 discusses investment risk and the importance of diversifying. In most situations, someone holding shares after exercising an ISO has more exposure to stock of that company than is healthy. Cash raised by selling some of the shares for AMT credit balancing can be used to make other investments that lower the overall risk of your portfolio.

AMT credit balancing ratios

AMT affects different people different ways, depending on various factors such as filing status, number of dependents, and itemized deductions. For most people, the only way to find the balancing point for AMT credit is to do an individualized tax projection. If your option profit is extremely large, however, the bulk of the profit may be taxed at the highest rates, making these individual factors relatively unimportant. In this case we can make at least a rough estimate of where your AMT credit balancing point will occur based on the top tax rates.

If your only truly large source of income is from exercising ISOs, the AMT credit balancing point occurs when the percentage of shares you hold is equal to the (a) the difference between the highest regular income tax rate and the 28% AMT rate, divided by (b) the difference between the highest regular income tax rate and the highest rate on long-term capital gain. Prior to 2013, when the highest regular tax rate was 35% and the capital gain rate was 15%, the result was 35% (7% divided by 20%). That means someone with $5 million in ISO profit could have sold 65% of the shares immediately after exercising the option without forgoing any tax benefit. The tax benefit maxed out when they held 35% of the shares.

Today's top rates are higher. AMT remains at 28%, but the highest regular income tax rate is 39.6% and we now have a 20% capital gains rate. If we perform the same calculation using these rates (rounding the regular rate to 40%), we get a "hold" percentage of 60% (12% divided by 20%). By this calculation you might want to sell only 40% of the shares immediately after exercising the option.

However, this calculation does not take state income tax into account. If you pay 10% state income tax on your option income, and claim that payment as an itemized deduction, the top effective rate of tax on ordinary income is 36%, not 40%. In this case your "hold" percentage scales back from 60% to 40%. In other words, the figures reverse, and your optimal strategy may be to sell about 60% of the shares and hold about 40%.

Effect of other income. The ratios described above are built on the implicit assumption that your ISO profit is quite large, and your other income fills in some or all of the lower tax brackets without greatly exceeding the amount that would get you to the top tax bracket. The ratios change if your other income is also very large.

> **Example:** You have $5 million in ISO profit and also $3 million in profit from nonqualified options, and your "hold" percentage based on federal and state income tax rates is 40%. In this case, because you have a large amount of other income that's taxed at the maximum rates, the 40% "hold" percentage applies to the $8 million total, not just the $5 million ISO profit. AMT credit balancing will occur at roughly the point where you hold ISO stock representing $3.2 million in ISO profit.

Caveats. Some caveats are in order. The accuracy of these estimates depends on the size of the option profit, with the accuracy diminishing as the profit becomes smaller. In any event, they're only estimates. They're offered to give you a rough idea what to expect if your option profit is very large, and not as a substitute for detailed planning. Also, you should bear in mind that the optimal tax strategy may expose you to more investment risk than is wise. Don't let these tax calculations talk you into a strategy that isn't suitable for you.

Recovering AMT Credit

Even knowledgeable planners have been known to make mistakes in dealing with the AMT credit.

> **Example:** You exercised an incentive stock option the previous year and sold the stock this year. Preliminary calculations indicate you won't make full use of your AMT credit this year despite selling all the stock. Your financial advisor points out that you can recover more of the credit if you exercise some nonqualified stock options. The added income will be taxed at about 35% under the regular tax and 28% under the AMT, so increasing your income by $100,000 will allow you to claim about $7,000 more of your AMT credit.

Let's assume for the moment that you don't have independent reasons for wanting to exercise the nonqualified stock options. The only reason you're considering this strategy is to recover more of your AMT credit. Does this make sense?

Absolutely not! This strategy doesn't reduce your tax in the year you exercise the nonqualified stock options. In fact, it increases your tax. Planners sometimes seem to think the benefit of "recovering" the AMT credit outweighs the detriment of paying tax sooner than necessary on the nonqualified stock options. Yet you didn't really *recover* anything. You *burned up* some or all of your remaining AMT credit, which would have been just as valuable in a later year. What's worse, your planning caused you to pay additional tax in the year you exercised the nonqualified stock options. You used taxes to reduce a tax benefit, instead of using a tax benefit to reduce taxes.

A strategy designed to recover AMT credit doesn't necessarily lower your taxes.

179

Gifting mature ISO shares

Savvy taxpayers know it can make sense to use appreciated stock—stock that has gone up in value—to make gifts. Giving shares to your children can make it possible to sell the shares at a lower tax cost. Donating the shares to charity can make it possible to eliminate tax on the gain altogether, while allowing you to claim a charitable contribution deduction for the full value.

> There are limitations on this deduction, so check the rules before proceeding.

It's usually a big mistake to use immature ISO shares to make family or charitable gifts. As we saw in Chapter 15, the tax consequences of this type of disqualifying disposition can be worse than for a sale of shares. After you satisfy the special holding period for ISO shares, though, you may want to consider gifting them. You should be aware that the tax benefit of doing so may not be as large as you would expect.

To understand why, keep in mind that the reason for gifting appreciated stock is to reduce or eliminate the tax you would pay if you sold the shares. If you're eligible to claim an AMT credit that will reduce or eliminate the tax you would pay on a sale of the shares, there may be little or no additional tax benefit in using these shares to make a gift. You may end up in the same situation as if you sold the shares, made a gift of the cash proceeds, and used the AMT credit to eliminate any tax you incurred on the sale.

You aren't necessarily shooting yourself in the foot with this planning idea. In fact, you may benefit from this strategy if you're able to recover most or all of your AMT credit without selling the shares, or if the stock's value went up after you exercised the option. Make sure you understand the overall effect on your tax situation, though. If you go into the transaction expecting a big tax benefit because the shares are appreciated, you may be disappointed.

State taxes

There are two important reasons to think about state income tax when you plan for the exercise of incentive stock options. The first is that some states have their own alternative minimum tax. If you live in California, for example, you can expect to pay a hefty amount of state AMT on top of federal AMT when you exercise an incentive stock option.

You also need to think about state taxes as they affect your federal AMT. State taxes are deductible if you itemize, but the deduction isn't allowed for AMT purposes. Proper timing of the payment of state taxes can reduce the amount of AMT you pay, or increase the amount of AMT that qualifies for the AMT credit. You may not have a lot of control over when you pay your state income taxes, but to the extent you have a choice you may save money if you time those payments for maximum advantage in connection with the federal AMT.

Part VI
Using Stock to Exercise Options

20

Using Stock to Exercise Nonqualified Options

This approach can save money if you would otherwise have to sell shares at a gain to raise money needed to exercise your stock nonqualified stock option.

SOME COMPANIES PERMIT OPTION HOLDERS to use shares of stock they already own to pay the purchase price when they exercise an option to buy new shares.

> **Example:** You have an option to buy 600 shares of stock for $5 per share. The current value of the stock is $12 per share. To exercise the option you can pay $3,000 in cash—or, if your company permits, you can "pay" $3,000 in stock. You would turn in 250 shares (250 times the current value of $12 equals $3,000) and receive 600 shares (an increase of 350 shares).

This form of exercise can be convenient because it relieves the option holder of the need to come up with cash to pay the exercise price. (Cash will still be required to cover withholding and other tax liabilities, however.) In addition, the tax results may be favorable when compared to an alternative where you sell stock to come up with the cash to exercise your option.

Availability

Not all companies permit this form of exercise. The company may not like this approach because it puts fewer shares in the hands of option holders compared to a cash exercise. The board of directors may believe that a cash exercise shows more commitment or has greater integrity. Whatever the reason, you can't *assume* this method of exercise is available. Read your option agreement and the stock option plan under which it was issued, and ask the appropriate person at your company if you're still unsure.

Of course this method of exercise isn't available if you don't own stock in the company. In that case you'll need to use cash, at least for your first purchase. After that you may be able to use stock you bought from an earlier exercise of an option to exercise later options. Be sure to understand the tax consequences before adopting this approach.

Certification instead of exchange

You might wonder whether it's necessary to have an actual exchange of shares. After all, the shares you receive in the exchange are identical to the shares you surrender. If you're going to turn in 250 shares to receive 600 that are exactly the same, why not just hold onto the 250 shares and receive 350 new shares?

In private letter rulings, the IRS has said you can do exactly that. The rulings describe a process in which you certify that you own the shares that are needed for the exchange. If the shares are held by a registered securities broker in street name on your behalf, you would submit a notarized statement attesting to the number of shares owned. If you hold the certificates yourself, you would submit the certificate numbers, which can be checked against the records of the transfer agent. The IRS says this is good enough to count as constructive delivery of the shares.

If available, this approach can save time and money in situations where it may be costly to actually tender the shares. If you're using the shares as collateral for a loan, for example, you may need the lender's permission to transfer the shares. In any event, the paperwork involved in the certification process is likely to be less cumbersome than tendering the shares.

Tax consequences

The tax consequences when you use stock to exercise a nonqualified option are unusual and interesting. You're treated as if two separate things happened:

- You made a *tax-free exchange* of old shares for an equal number of new shares (the "exchange shares"), *and*

- You received *additional* shares (the "added shares") for zero payment.

As to the *exchange* shares you don't report any income, or any capital gain. The shares you receive in the exchange have the same basis and holding period as the shares you turned in. It's as if you simply continued to hold the old shares.

As to the *added* shares, you have to report the value as compensation income when you receive them (or when they vest, if later), the same as if you received a grant or award of stock, as explained in Chapter 8. Those shares take a basis equal to the amount of compensation income you report, and your holding period begins when you acquire them (or when they vest).

Example: You have an option to buy 600 shares of stock for $5 per share (a total of $3,000). You exercise the option by turning in 250 shares worth $12 per share. Assuming the shares are vested when you receive them, you would end up with 250 shares that have the same basis and holding period as the shares you turned in, plus 350 shares with a basis of $12 per share and a holding period that begins when you acquire the shares.

Identification. When you decide to sell some of your shares, it will be important to determine which shares you want to sell. In some cases you'll want to sell the newer shares because they have a higher basis. In other cases you may want to sell the older shares to get long-term gain instead of short-term gain. Be sure you understand the principles and procedures for identifying shares as explained in Chapter 6.

Using ISO shares. It may be possible to use shares you own from a previous exercise of an incentive stock option to pay the purchase price on exercise of a nonqualified stock option. This exchange will not be treated as a disposition of the ISO stock, but the exchange shares will *continue* to be ISO shares. That means a subsequent sale of those shares may cause you to report compensation income if you haven't satisfied the special holding period. In the example above, if you turned in 250 ISO shares, then 250 of the shares you received in the exchange would be treated as ISO shares with the same basis and holding period as the shares you turned in.

> **Caution:** The same rule doesn't apply if you use ISO shares to exercise an ISO. Chapter 21 explains the rules for using stock to exercise an ISO.

Evaluation

This method of exercising an option doesn't produce any magical benefits. The greatest advantage is where you would have to sell stock you already own in order to come up with the money you need to exercise the option. In this case, using stock to exercise the option permits you to avoid reporting gain from a sale of those shares. But you'll report the gain eventually, so this is a tax deferral, not a tax reduction.

If one of the alternatives available to you is combined exercise and sale (or *cashless exercise*), as explained in Chapter 13, you should find that the method described in this chapter has almost exactly the same consequences—provided that you sold only enough of the newly purchased shares to pay the exercise price. Normally, the sale portion of that transaction produces very little gain or loss, and you end up holding the same number of shares (and reporting the same amount of income) as if you had used stock to exercise your option.

Of course, you don't necessarily have to use either of these "cashless" methods to exercise your option. You can use funds you have available from another source—savings, perhaps, or taking out a loan—to exercise the option. Comparing this alternative to a "cashless" exercise is an investment question. Do you want to maximize your holding in the company's stock? If so, use cash from another source to exercise your option. If not, consider a cashless form of exercise, if the company makes it available.

21

Using Stock to Exercise ISOs

Avoid this approach if you're turning in immature ISO or ESPP shares. Even if you're using other shares, this strategy isn't for you unless you understand these complicated rules and feel confident you won't make a disqualifying disposition.

REGULATIONS ISSUED IN 2004 lay out the tax consequences when you use stock to exercise an incentive stock option. This technique is definitely not for everybody. The rules are so complicated that it may be difficult to figure out if you'll end up with a net benefit. What's worse, if you make a disqualifying disposition after using stock to exercise an ISO, these rules can leave you with a result that's unexpected and unfair.

Source of the old stock

The tax consequences of this form of exercise depend on whether or not you use *immature stock* to exercise the option. You have immature stock if you acquired the stock by exercising an incentive stock option or by purchase under a qualified employee stock purchase plan and haven't yet satisfied the special holding period (the later of two years after option grant or one year after exercise). If you're *not* using immature stock to pay for the shares you're buying, the shares you're using can be any of the following:

- *Mature* ISO or ESPP stock (in other words, stock you acquired by exercising an incentive stock option or by purchase under a qualified ESPP long enough ago that you've satisfied the special ISO holding period).

- Stock from exercising nonqualified stock options.

- Stock acquired in any other way, including purchases on the open market.

Using shares other than immature ISO shares

Generally, if you're going to use stock to exercise an ISO, you want to use shares *other than* immature stock. Here are the *regular tax* consequences when you do so:

- For regular tax purposes, you don't report any income on the exercise of the incentive stock option. (This rule is the same as if you used cash to exercise your option.)

- You don't report any gain or loss on the shares you used to pay the purchase price on the option. That's because you've made a tax-free exchange of those shares for ISO shares.

- The shares you receive are divided into two batches. One batch includes a number of shares equal to the number of shares you turned in (the *exchange shares*). The other group includes all the additional shares you received (the *added shares*).

- The exchange shares have the same basis as the shares you turned in. They also have the same holding period as the shares you turned in—but only for purposes of determining whether any capital gain or loss on a sale is long-term. For purposes of determining whether you've satisfied the special ISO holding period, your holding period for these shares begins on the date you exercise the option.

- The added shares have a basis equal to the amount of cash (if any) you paid to exercise the option. This amount may be zero or close to zero because you used stock to pay most or all of the exercise price. These shares have a holding period that begins when you receive them.

- Both the exchange shares and the added shares are subject to the rules that cause you to report compensation income if you make a *disqualifying disposition* before satisfying the special ISO holding period.

AMT consequences. The IRS hasn't spelled out the consequences under the alternative minimum tax in as great detail as the regular tax consequences. The following results would be consistent with the approach the IRS has taken in this area:

- When you use stock to exercise an ISO, you have to report an AMT adjustment in the same amount as if you had used cash to exercise the option.

- The exchange shares have the same AMT basis as the shares you used to pay the exercise price.

- The added shares have an AMT basis equal to the amount of cash you paid (if any) *plus* the amount of the AMT adjustment.

Using immature shares

Because of a special rule—sometimes called the *anti-pyramid rule*—it's generally undesirable to use immature stock to exercise an incentive stock option. Here's what happens:

- For regular income tax purposes, you don't report any income on the exercise of the new ISO.

- However, *you've made a disqualifying disposition of the immature stock you turned in.* That means you have to report compensation income. If you used immature ISO stock, the compensation income is equal to the bargain element from the exercise of the *old* ISO (the one you exercised to acquire the immature ISO stock). You can't reduce the amount you report as compensation income even if the stock has declined in value since the date of the previous option exercise. If you used immature ESPP stock, apply the early disposition rules described in Chapter 27.

- At the same time, the disposition of the immature stock is treated in part as a tax-free exchange. So apart from the compensation income you report as described above, you don't report gain or loss on the exchange of old shares for new ISO shares, even if the stock has gone up in value since you acquired it.

- The shares you receive are divided into two groups. One group includes a number of shares equal to the number of shares you turned in (the *exchange shares*). The other group includes all the additional shares you received (the *added shares*).

- The exchange shares have the same basis as the shares you turned in, increased by the amount of compensation income reported because of the disqualifying disposition. They also have the same holding period as the shares you turned in— but only for purposes of determining whether any capital gain or loss on a sale is long-term. For purposes of determining whether you've satisfied the special ISO holding period, your holding period for these shares begins on the date you exercise the new ISO.

- The added shares have a basis equal to the amount of cash (if any) paid to exercise the option. This may be zero or close to zero because you used stock to pay most or all of the exercise price. These shares have a holding period that begins on the date you exercised the new ISO.

- Both the exchange shares and the added shares are subject to rules requiring you to report compensation income if you make a disqualifying disposition.

AMT consequences. The following description of alternative minimum tax consequences would be consistent with the approach the IRS has taken in this area:

- You have to report an AMT adjustment on the exercise of the new ISO in the same amount as if you had used cash to exercise the option.

- The exchange shares have the same AMT basis as the shares you used to pay the exercise price, increased, only in the case of immature ESPP shares, by the amount of compensation income reported on the exchange. (The AMT basis of the shares you used to pay the exercise price already included the bargain element from exercise of the original ISO.)

- The added shares have an AMT basis equal to the amount of cash you paid (if any) *plus* the amount of the AMT adjustment.

> Overall these rules are quite unfavorable. It would rarely make sense to use immature shares to pay the exercise price when exercising an ISO.

Disqualifying dispositions

For a long time we had no official guidance to tell us what happens if you use stock to exercise an incentive stock option and subsequently make a disqualifying disposition. The good news is that the Treasury finally adopted regulations dealing with this topic in 2004. The bad news is that they blew a chance to give us a sensible set of rules. Under these regs you can end up reporting compensation income that exceeds your profit from the option, even if your disqualifying disposition is a sale that qualifies for the income limitation rule. You can sell half the shares and have to report compensation income that's much more than half the bargain element of the option you exercised, although you retain the other shares long enough to satisfy the special holding period. In short the rules are highly unfavorable. In light of these rules, I recommend against using stock to exercise an incentive stock option except when you're confident you won't make a disqualifying disposition.

One feature of the rules is a requirement to treat any disqualifying disposition as if it comes first from the shares that have the lowest basis. Generally, when you use stock to exercise an incentive stock option, you end up with exchange shares that have the same basis as the shares you turned in, and added shares that have *zero* basis. That means you start out selling shares with no basis at all, taking the maximum tax hit. You get this result even if you actually sell the exchange shares (the ones with higher basis) before you sell the added shares.

> **Example:** You have an incentive stock option to buy 100 shares at $10 per share. You also have some shares you bought earlier at a price of $5 per share. When the stock is trading at $25, you use 40 of those older shares to pay the $1,000 exercise price of the ISO. As a result you hold 40 exchange shares and 60 added shares. Your bargain element at the time of exercise is $1,500 (100 shares times $15 per share, the difference between the $25 value of the shares and the $10 exercise price).
>
> Less than a year later, you sell 75 of these shares for $30 per share. You're automatically treated as selling the 60 added shares first. Those shares have zero basis, so you report $1,800 of profit on those shares, consisting of $1,500 of compensation income and $300 of capital gain. You also have to report gain on the 15 exchange shares you sold.

Notice that you've reported all the compensation income from the option even though you still hold 25 of the shares. Furthermore, it appears that under these rules you would have to report compensation income even if you sold the shares at $10 per share (the same price you paid as the exercise price of the option), even though you don't have any profit when you sell at that price.

> These rules can produce truly evil results. Don't use stock to exercise an ISO unless you're confident that you'll be able to avoid a disqualifying disposition.

Part VII
Vesting

General Rules for Vesting

Here's a closer look at some rules we outlined earlier.

IT'S UNFORTUNATE, BUT one of the most important issues relating to equity compensation is a somewhat technical one that uses arcane terminology. The basic idea here is fairly simple, though. If the company puts certain kinds of restrictions on your right to keep the stock, you don't have full ownership of it yet. That means you don't report income from receiving the stock until the restrictions go away.

Terminology

Here are some words you need to know in working with the vesting rules:

Substantial risk of forfeiture. Only certain types of restrictions will delay the reporting of income. In tax lingo, these are restrictions that create a *substantial risk of forfeiture.*

Vested. If your stock is subject to a substantial risk of forfeiture *and* is not transferable, we say it isn't *vested*. So these are two ways of saying the same thing: if it isn't vested, you have a substantial risk of forfeiture. If you don't have a substantial risk of forfeiture (or the stock is transferable), your stock is vested.

Lapse and nonlapse restrictions. The regulations distinguish between two kinds of restrictions, and give them different tax treatment. Your stock is subject to a *nonlapse restriction* if three things are true:

- The restriction requires you to sell (or offer to sell) your property under a formula price. For example, it may require you to sell for book value, or a multiple of sales or profits.

- The restriction will never go away.

- If you sell or otherwise transfer the stock to someone else, the restriction will apply to that person as well.

Any restriction that doesn't meet the requirements described above is a *lapse restriction*. Notice that a restriction can be permanent and still be a lapse restriction under this definition. Permanency is only one of the requirements for a nonlapse restriction.

Substantial risk of forfeiture

There's much confusion about what constitutes a *substantial risk of forfeiture*. Only certain types of risks count here. You may receive stock under circumstances where there's a very real risk that you won't ever get to sell the stock at its current value. Nevertheless, if the risk isn't a substantial risk of forfeiture, you still have to report compensation income *now*. You can't wait until the risk goes away.

Generally, you have a risk of forfeiture under these rules when your right to continue owning the stock depends on whether you continue to work for the company. The most common situation by far is where the company says you'll forfeit the stock (or have to sell it back for less than full value) if your employment terminates before a specified amount of time has elapsed.

A risk of forfeiture doesn't have to relate to a specific time period. For example, it might say you'll have permanent ownership of the stock when sales for your division reach a certain level. You can also have a risk of forfeiture based on an agreement not to compete. Perhaps you received stock in connection with termination of your employment, subject to forfeiture if you work for a competitor of the company within the next two years.

Bear in mind that the risk of forfeiture has to be *substantial*. If it's obvious that the condition for permanent ownership of the stock will be satisfied, the condition doesn't create a substantial risk of forfeiture. Same thing if there's good reason to believe the company won't enforce the forfeiture provision (for example, you control the company). An agreement not to compete may not create a substantial risk of forfeiture if you've reached retirement age or for some other reason have no real ability to compete.

Risk of decline in value

A risk that the stock will decline in value is *not* a substantial risk of forfeiture. This is a hard fact for many people to accept, especially if they're unable to sell the stock. You may have a situation where you can't sell the stock for a period of time, and you believe there's a risk the value of the company will decline before you can make a sale. With limited exceptions described in Chapter 23 on restrictions under the securities laws, you don't have a substantial risk of forfeiture in these circumstances. You have to report the current value of the stock as compensation income.

Rules for vesting

The rules for vesting depend on whether you make the section 83b election. The material in this chapter assumes you did *not* make this election. Chapter 24 provides details concerning the section 83b election.

General. The tax law treats you as if you don't really own stock that isn't vested. You don't report income when you receive the stock. The time before the stock vested doesn't count for purposes of determining whether you have long-term capital gain or loss when you sell the stock. In other words, your holding period begins when the stock vests, not when you received the stock. What's more, if the stock pays dividends, you report compensation income, not dividend income, for any dividends you receive before the stock vests.

Forfeitures. If you fail to satisfy the conditions that create the risk of forfeiture, you forfeit the stock. No doubt you will consider that an economic loss. The stock was yours, and had value, and now it isn't yours any more. As a general rule, though, you can't claim a loss on your tax return. The tax law treats you as if you don't own the stock, and you can't claim a loss for something you don't own.

There's an exception to this rule. If you paid something for the stock, and didn't get that amount back at the time of the forfeiture (or got only part of it back) you can report a loss. This would be an unusual situation, because most companies won't ask you to forfeit the money you came up with to acquire the stock.

Vesting. If things go well, you'll satisfy the conditions to have unrestricted ownership of the stock. At that point the stock is *vested*. You report compensation income at that time, regardless of whether you sell the stock. The amount of income is the value of the stock at the time it vested, reduced by the amount (if any) you paid for the stock.

From that point on, you're treated as if you bought the stock on the date it vested. Even though you may have held the stock for years, you'll have short-term gain or loss if you sell the stock a year or less after the vesting date. You have to hold the stock *more than a year after the vesting date* to be able to report long-term capital gain when you sell it.

The *amount* of gain or loss when you sell the stock depends on your *basis* for the stock. Your basis includes the amount of income you report when the stock vests. If you paid anything for the stock, that's included in your basis, too. So your basis is the amount (if any) paid for the stock, increased by the amount of income you report when the stock vests.

23

Vesting and Securities Rules

Your shares may be vested for tax purposes even though you're prevented from selling them.

IT'S POSSIBLE YOU'LL FIND YOURSELF holding shares of stock you can't sell, at least for the time being, because of restrictions imposed by the securities laws. That's an awkward position to be in if you have to report income, and pay tax, when you receive your shares. You're likely to wonder if you can postpone reporting the income until the restriction lapses and you're able to sell the stock. With very limited exceptions, the answer is no.

Section 16b

One type of restriction is the *short swing profits rule* imposed by Section 16b of the Securities Exchange Act of 1934. Under this rule you may be required to give up any profits realized from a sale of stock that occurs within six months of a purchase. This rule *does* delay vesting for tax purposes, when it applies. But it doesn't apply very often.

For one thing, Section 16b applies only to certain officers, directors and major shareholders of companies required to file reports to the SEC. That's a small fraction of the people who receive equity compensation. If you're one of those people, you'll know it because the company's legal counsel will have informed you of things you must do—and things you must not.

Even if you find yourself on this short list, you may never have to deal with Section 16b in connection with your equity compensation. One reason is that under Section 16b—unlike the tax law—your holding period begins when you *receive* an option, not when you *exercise* it. If you hold an option for at least six months before you exercise it, you've already satisfied the Section 16b holding period when you receive the stock. What's more, the Section 16b regulations provide that most grants of equity compensation are exempt from the six-month holding period.

The bottom line is that Section 16b applies to relatively few people and, when it comes to equity compensation, applies in relatively few situations.

Rule 144

Now we turn to a rule that applies to *many* people who receive equity compensation. If you receive unregistered stock in a public corporation, you're likely to be required to sign an *investment letter* saying you're acquiring the stock for investment and not for resale. The stock certificate will be stamped with a legend indicating it can be sold only in accordance with certain requirements. This stock may be called *lettered stock,* or *Rule 144 stock.*

What's going on here? Companies have to comply with an elaborate (and expensive) registration requirement to bring stock to the market. This assures that investors have access to information that will enable them to make an informed decision on whether to buy the stock. The SEC doesn't want companies to sidestep this process by issuing shares to persons affiliated with the company when those people are going to turn around and sell the shares on the market. Rule 144 establishes rules under which affiliated individuals can receive, and eventually (but not immediately) sell, unregistered shares.

The problem here is that Rule 144 does *not* prevent your stock from being vested under the tax law. Why not? Perhaps because Rule 144 isn't an absolute prohibition on sale. You can't sell your stock on the open market, but you're permitted to arrange a private sale if you can find a buyer who will accept the stock subject to the restrictions of Rule 144.

Then again, a Rule 144 restriction doesn't impose a risk that you'll lose the stock. Your risk is that the stock will decline in value. But the tax regulations specify that a risk of decline in value isn't a substantial risk of forfeiture.

There's one case in which a Rule 144 restriction—coupled with an *additional* restriction imposed by the company—satisfied the court that stock should not be considered vested for tax purposes. I'm not inclined to rely on that case, however. It isn't clear to me that other courts, including the Tax Court, would follow this holding outside the New England states that are included in the First Circuit.

Generally, then, you can't use a Section 144 restriction to delay vesting. You also can't use it to reduce the value of the stock, even though you'll surely have to settle for a discount if you make a private sale before the end of the Rule 144 holding period. About all you can do with Rule 144 is grin and bear it.

Blackout Periods

Many companies impose *blackout periods* in which employees aren't permitted to trade in the company's stock. These periods are timed in relation to the company's quarterly reports. The securities laws don't exactly require blackout periods, but a company that doesn't impose them risks violations. They avoid the implication that employees used inside information to get the better of public investors who don't yet have access to that information. Blackout periods help assure the integrity of the market in the company's stock and can help avoid lawsuits from unhappy investors.

The courts have ruled against taxpayers who argued that a blackout period delays vesting. The regulations state that property is vested for tax purposes when it is *either* transferable *or* not subject to a substantial risk of forfeiture. It seems reasonably clear that a restriction on transferability, by itself, will not prevent vesting. You need, in addition, a substantial risk of forfeiture. As noted earlier, the regulations plainly state that the risk of property declining in value is *not* a substantial risk of forfeiture. Conclusion: blackout periods don't delay vesting.

Lockup periods

A similar issue arises as to *lockup periods*. These are periods in which some or all of the existing shareholders are not permitted to sell shares after a company goes public. The securities laws don't impose this requirement; a lockup is imposed by underwriters to make it easier to sell shares that are being offered to the public. As in the case of blackout periods, the reasoning used above implies that lockups (without some other restriction) don't delay vesting.

Perspective

I hear a lot of frustration from people who feel they shouldn't have to report income from their stock until such time as they're free to sell it on the open market. I sympathize with that feeling. At the same time, there are plenty of people out there who receive stock in companies that aren't publicly traded. Some of these people have no reasonable prospect of selling their stock in the near future, yet they have to report income equal to the value of the stock when they receive it. The point: the tax applies because you received something of value, *not* because you received something you can immediately sell. If you have to pay tax on receiving property you can't sell, you're in an uncomfortable position—but not a unique one.

24

Section 83b Election

Here's a closer look at when the section 83b election makes sense, and how to it.

THE TAX RULES FOR STOCK THAT ISN'T VESTED provide both an advantage and a disadvantage when compared to the rules for vested stock. You get the advantage of waiting until the restriction lapses before you report income. If the stock goes up in value while you're waiting, though, you'll report *more* income. A large increase in the value of your stock prior to vesting can have painful tax consequences.

If you don't like the trade-off, you can change the rules. To do this, you file the section 83b election. When you do, you'll be treated (mostly) as if you received vested stock. But you have to act fast: *the election must be made within 30 days after you receive the stock.*

Availability

The election is available when you receive stock with delayed vesting. The point of the election is to treat the stock as if it's already vested, so there's no need to file it if you receive stock that's immediately vested. You might have a situation where it isn't clear whether the stock is vested. In this case you might want to file the election just to eliminate any doubt.

The election is *not* available for *options*. With very limited exceptions, options don't produce current compensation income even if they're vested. Filing a section 83b election when you receive an option doesn't cause you to report current income and, more importantly, doesn't eliminate compensation income when you exercise the option. The election simply doesn't apply to options.

It may apply when you exercise an option, however. Some options impose restrictions so that the stock isn't vested right away when you receive it. In this case it may make sense to file the section 83b election when you exercise the option. See Chapter 25.

Effect of the election

If you make the section 83b election, you report compensation income when you receive the stock, not when it vests. The value of the stock is determined when you receive it. You have nothing to report at the time the stock vests.

> **Example:** In return for services, you receive 4,000 shares of stock in a startup company. When you receive the stock it isn't vested, and the value is $1.25 per share. Shortly thereafter the company goes public and is hugely successful. When the shares vest two years later they're trading at $50.
>
> Without the section 83b election, you'll report nothing when you receive the shares. When the stock vests, it's worth $200,000 and you'll report that much compensation

income. You may pay $70,000 or more in federal income tax as a result.

The result is very different if you file the section 83b election. You would report $5,000 of compensation income when you receive the stock. You have nothing to report when the stock vests. You can continue to hold it without paying another dime of tax. If you sell the stock for $200,000, you'll have a long-term capital gain of $195,000. The tax rate will be much lower, and your total tax will be greatly reduced.

Each rose has its thorns

The section 83b election doesn't always work out this well. If the stock doesn't rise in value after you make the election, you've *accelerated* tax (paid it sooner) without receiving any benefit. If the stock goes down, you've paid *more* tax than would have been necessary.

Worse, you might forfeit the stock after making the election. In this case you would claim a capital loss for any unrecovered portion of the amount you actually paid for the stock (if any), but you would get no deduction relative to the compensation income you reported when you made the election. That's a miserable result: the election caused you to pay tax on income you didn't get to keep, with no offsetting tax benefit later on.

When the election makes sense

The section 83b election makes sense in the following situations:

- The amount of income you'll report when you make the election is small and the potential growth in value of the stock is great, or

- You expect reasonable growth in the value of the stock and the likelihood of a forfeiture is very small.

Conversely, you should avoid the section 83b election where a forfeiture seems likely, or where you'll pay a great deal of tax at the time of the election with only modest prospects for growth in the value of the stock.

Don't miss this chance. You might have to accept a risk of forfeiture on your stock even though you paid full value when you received it. The way this usually works is you agree to sell the stock back for the amount you paid if you quit within a specified period. This is a risk of forfeiture even though you won't lose your original investment. The risk is that you'll lose part of the value of the stock if your employment terminates before the stock vests. *That means that if the stock goes up in value, you'll report compensation income when the stock vests.*

You can avoid this result by making the section 83b election when you buy the stock. In this situation *the election is free.* The election costs nothing because the amount of income you report is the value of the stock minus the amount you paid. You paid full value, so the amount of income is zero. Failure to make this free election can be a costly mistake.

Preparing the election

There's no special form to use in making the election. However, the IRS offers a suggested (not required) format for preparing it. Their sample election (from Rev. Proc. 2012-29) appears at the end of this chapter.

Filing the election

The key point about filing the election has already been mentioned. At risk of repeating myself: *the election has to be filed within 30 days after you receive the property.* If you don't act within that time you're out of luck. You can't wait until you file your return. Here's what you need to do:

- Within 30 days after you receive the stock, send the election to the IRS office where you file your income tax return. (Check the instructions for Form 1040 if you're not sure of the address.) *I highly recommend sending this election by certified mail and getting a stamped receipt with a legible date.*

- Provide a copy of the election to the company that granted the stock.

- In the unusual situation where you had the company transfer the stock to someone other than yourself (such as a trustee), you need to provide a copy to that person as well.

- Attach a copy of the election when you file your income tax return for that year.

> People sometimes forget one or more of these steps and wonder if their election is still valid. It's likely (though not certain) that the IRS will treat an election as valid once you've filed it with the IRS within the 30-day period, even if you failed to follow through with the other requirements.

This is one of those situations where it's very important to keep good records. Make sure you maintain a copy of the election, and evidence that you filed it within the time limit. The value of the stock—and the importance of this election—could grow substantially during the time it takes for the stock to vest.

Section 83(b) Election

The undersigned taxpayer hereby elects, pursuant to § 83(b) of the Internal Revenue Code of 1986, as amended, to include in gross income as compensation for services the excess (if any) of the fair market value of the shares described below over the amount paid for those shares.

1. The name, taxpayer identification number, address of the undersigned, and the taxable year for which this election is being made are:

    TAXPAYER'S NAME: _____
    TAXPAYER'S SSN: _____
    ADDRESS: _____
    TAXABLE YEAR: Calendar Year 20__

2. The property which is the subject of this election is _____ shares of common stock of _____.

3. The property was transferred to the undersigned on [DATE].

4. The property is subject to the following restrictions: [Describe applicable restrictions here.]

5. The fair market value of the property at the time of transfer (determined without regard to any restriction other than a nonlapse restriction as defined in § 1.83-3(h) of the Income Tax Regulations) is: $_____ per share x _____ shares = $_____.

6. For the property transferred, the undersigned paid $_____ per share x _____ shares = $_____.

7. The amount to include in gross income is $_____. [The result of the amount reported in Item 5 minus the amount reported in Item 6.]

The undersigned taxpayer will file this election with the Internal Revenue Service office with which taxpayer files his or her annual income tax return not later than 30 days after the date of transfer of the property. A copy of the election also will be furnished to the person for whom the services were performed. Additionally, the undersigned will include a copy of the election with his or her income tax return for the taxable year in which the property is transferred. The undersigned is the person performing the services in connection with which the property was transferred.

Dated: _____   _____
                                              Taxpayer

25

"Early Exercise" Stock Option Plans

These plans allow you to exercise options before the stock is vested.

MOST STOCK OPTION PLANS PROVIDE FOR STAGED EXERCISE of options. In a typical arrangement, you have to wait a year before you can exercise any of your options; at the end of a year, you can exercise 25%, then another year later you qualify to exercise another 25% and so on.

There's a more flexible approach used by a number of companies, especially startups that are planning to go public. These arrangements permit you to exercise your options whenever you want. If you exercise early, however, your stock isn't vested right away. You may be forced to sell it back to the company at your original purchase price if your employment terminates within a specified time. Vesting of the stock may be staged in a manner similar to the exercise of options under a more traditional plan—say, 25% per year over four years. Plans with this feature are called *early exercise* stock option plans.

If you hold onto your options until the stock is vested, this type of plan will provide the same economic and tax consequences as a normal stock option plan. You have another alternative, though. You can exercise your options *before* the stock is vested. That choice can produce big tax savings, but exposes you to economic and tax risks. The company may not pull off the planned IPO, leaving you with shares for which there is no market. Your employment may terminate, permitting the company to buy back the shares at the price you paid under the option. In either case, you may not be able to recover any tax you paid in connection with the early exercise of your option.

Planning considerations depend on whether you hold nonqualified stock options or incentive stock options. For nonquals, it wouldn't make sense to exercise your option early unless you also intend to file the section 83b election. For ISOs, you might file the section 83b election (and would certainly do so if you exercised the option before the price of the stock rose above the exercise price of the option), but it can also make sense to exercise an ISO before the stock is vested *without* making this election. You can start the clock running on the special holding period to avoid a disqualifying disposition, while postponing the AMT consequences of exercising the option until the year the stock vests.

Nonqualified stock options

Early exercise plans are designed to permit you to exercise options at a time when the stock you receive isn't *vested.* Unless you file the section 83b election at the time you exercise a nonqualified stock option, you'll report income at the time the stock vests. More importantly, the *amount* of income you report will be based on the value of the stock when it vests. If the value of the stock goes up rapidly between the time you exercise the option and the time the stock vests, you'll report a great deal of compensation income on the vesting date.

These plans are designed with the idea that you may want to exercise the option before the stock has gone up very much—perhaps even immediately after you receive the option. And the expectation is that you'll file the section 83b election. The plan or the option may even *require* you to file the section 83b election when you exercise. That way, you report income at the time you exercise the option—and you won't be hit with a huge tax liability when the stock vests.

> **Example:** You received a nonqualified option to buy 10,000 shares at $0.50 when the company was in its infancy. Now things are looking good. The stock's value is $1, but it will zoom to $5 if the company secures another round of venture capital. In another 18 months the company may go public, and the stock could be at $20 or higher. That would give you a profit of close to $200,000.
>
> If you don't exercise until the stock is at $20, all that profit will be compensation income, taxed at the highest rates. Even if you exercise now, you may have to report most of your profit as compensation income if you don't make the section 83b election. But if you exercise now and make the election, you report only $5,000 of compensation income. Any future growth in the value of the stock will be capital gain. If you hold the stock more than a year, your capital gain will qualify for the favorable long-term rates. Potential tax savings: as much as $40,000 or more.

ISOs and early exercise plans

There's a twist on these rules if your option is an incentive stock option, rather than a nonqualified stock option. If we assume you're going to hold your shares long enough to avoid a disqualifying disposition, the fact that your stock isn't vested has no bearing on your regular income tax. You don't report income when you exercise an ISO, and you don't report income when the stock vests. Yet it's important that the stock isn't vested—and it may be important for you to do something about it.

If you hold ISO stock after the end of the year of exercise, the rules for alternative minimum tax treat you as if you exercised a nonqualified option. Under the regular tax, if you exercise a nonqualified option but the stock isn't vested, you don't report income at that time. You report income when the stock vests instead. The same principle applies to AMT treatment of exercise of an ISO.

At first blush that sounds like a good thing. AMT is bad, so why not put it off until another year? In some cases that's a good idea. But when you postpone the *income* from exercising your option, you postpone the *measurement* of that income.

> **Example:** Suppose you have an ISO to buy stock at $5 per share. When you exercise the option, the stock is valued at $6 per share. If the stock is vested at that time, you report an AMT adjustment of $1 per share. But let's assume the stock doesn't vest until a year later. During that time the company has gone public and the stock is worth $30 per share when it vests. Now you have to report an AMT adjustment of $25 per share. If you have a large number of shares, that's a big difference!

The IRS says in this situation you can file a *special* section 83b election just for purposes of the AMT. The election will work exactly the same way for the AMT as the regular section 83b election works under the regular tax. You'll report your AMT adjustment in the year you exercise the option, even though the stock won't vest until later. The amount of the adjustment will be determined as of the exercise date. You won't have anything to report at the time the stock vests.

That doesn't mean you always want to make this election if you exercise an incentive stock option before the stock is vested. If the stock price zoomed upward before you exercised the option, you could be facing a big AMT bill for the year of exercise if you file the election. You might be better off postponing the AMT liability until the year the stock vests—and eliminating the risk that you'll overpay AMT because of a decline in stock value during the vesting period, or because you forfeit the shares.

Special holding period. The rules of section 83 don't apply to stock that's been held for a qualifying sale after exercise of an ISO (see section 83(e)(1)), so it appears that the special holding period for ISO stock is measured without regard to the vesting date. In other words, you don't have to hold the shares more than a year after the vesting date if you meet the other requirements. Keep in mind, though, that you may have to hold the shares longer than normal. Recall that the shares have to be held more than a year after the exercise date *and* more than two years after the option grant date. If you exercise an ISO right after it's granted, you'll have to hold the shares two years to avoid a disqualifying disposition.

Disqualifying dispositions. What happens if you *do* have a disqualifying disposition? The law isn't exactly clear. The 2004 regulations on incentive stock options say that for purposes of the regular income tax you have to measure compensation income as of the vesting date. That's true even if you filed a section 83b election, because this election affects only AMT when it applies to shares from an incentive stock option. I believe there's a valid argument that the regulations are wrong on this point, and that compensation income should be measured as of the date the option was exercised.

Example: You exercise an incentive stock option, paying $2 per share at a time when that's the fair market value of the shares. You file a section 83b election for AMT purposes, reporting zero adjustment because you paid full value for the shares. The company has a successful IPO and the shares are trading at $25 on the vesting date. You subsequently sell the shares at $37 in a disqualifying disposition (less than two years after the grant date of your stock option).

Under my interpretation of the law, your compensation income is measured as of the date of exercise for an incentive stock option, so you would report your entire profit from this sale as capital gain. According to the tax regulations, you have to measure compensation income as of the vesting date, and that means reporting $23 per share as compensation income with the rest of your profit being reported as capital gain. As a practical matter you'll have to follow the rule in the regulation unless you have enough money at stake to hire a lawyer and fight the issue in court—and even then there's no way to be sure which way the court will rule.

Exercise immediately?

Early exercise stock option plans invite you to consider the possibility of exercising your option immediately after you receive it. If you do this, your compensation income (or AMT adjustment) should be close to zero, because the exercise price is equal to fair market value at the time the option was granted. You can file the section 83b election (or special section 83b election) described above to avoid having to report any compensation income or AMT adjustment at the time the stock vests. If everything works right, you'll receive the full value of your option while reporting nothing but long-term capital gain. This is why early exercise plans are attractive to some companies, especially ones that are planning to go public.

Sound too good to be true? It isn't, really. To see why, think about what would have happened if your company offered you a different deal. Instead of an option, the company simply said you're allowed to buy some stock right now, paying fair market value, with the stock subject to restrictions so that it isn't vested. You would make the (regular) section 83b election to avoid having to report income when the stock vests. The election doesn't cost you anything because you paid full fair market value for the stock. Guess what? You would be in exactly the same situation as if you exercised an option under an early exercise stock option plan.

There really isn't any magic with this type of plan. In effect, if you exercise immediately you're giving up the benefit of holding an option: the ability to wait and see how the stock performs before exercising. For a mature company with a stock price established on the market, you wouldn't be interested in such an arrangement. You'd be better off buying the stock on the open market without any restriction.

The payoff comes with a company that isn't publicly traded. You don't have any way to buy the stock on the market because it isn't available. The only way you can get it is if the company offers you a deal. Getting the kind of a deal described here shortly before the company goes public can be a major bonanza. That's how Margaret Whitman, during her stint as CEO of eBay, Inc. reportedly put herself in a position to save over $100 million in taxes.

Of course you don't *have* to exercise your options immediately. Particularly if there's some doubt as to whether the company can pull off an IPO (or anything else that will make its value go up), you may want to wait and see. That's the benefit of an option: the ability to get a free look. There's a tax cost if you wait until after the value has gone up a great deal, though, so the "look" isn't completely free.

Part VIII
Employee Stock Purchase Plans

Overview of Employee Stock Purchase Plans

A good way to acquire stock in your company.

LET'S MAKE SURE WE'RE ON THE SAME PAGE. An employee stock purchase plan ("ESPP") is *not* the same as an employee stock ownership plan ("ESOP"). An ESOP is a retirement plan that invests in stock of the employer. This book doesn't cover retirement plans, so we won't be discussing ESOPs.

ESPPs offer a convenient way for you to invest in the stock of the company where you work. Many of these plans also offer a discount, making it possible to invest at a lower price than if you opened a brokerage account and bought shares in the stock market. The stock is held in a regular investment account, not a retirement account, but special rules may apply to a sale or other disposition if you bought the shares at a discount.

Two types of ESPP

ESPPs come in two flavors, qualified and nonqualified. We can draw a parallel with the difference between ISOs and nonqualified stock options:

- Qualified ESPPs, like ISO plans, have to meet special requirements set forth in the tax law.

- Having met those requirements, qualified ESPPs, like ISOs, can offer advantageous tax treatment to recipients of the benefits.

- Nonqualified ESPPs, like nonqualified stock options, do not have to meet any special requirements, and provide no special tax treatment to participants.

Qualified employee stock purchase plans are sometimes called *Section 423 plans*, referring to the section of the Internal Revenue Code that contains many of the rules for these plans.

ISO compared with ESPP

Some of the rules for qualified ESPPs are exactly the same as for incentive stock options, which are described in Part V of this book. In fact, the IRS sometimes lumps both benefits together under a single term: *statutory options*. Yet there are many important differences.

- Although ESPPs can offer options, more often they work as a way to sign up to buy shares through payroll deduction.

- An ISO has to be priced at or above the value of the stock as of the date the ISO is granted, but an ESPP can offer a discount of up to 15% from the value of the stock at the time the price is established.

▪ A company can offer ISOs to a select group of executives or other employees, but a qualified ESPP has to be available to *all* employees, with limited exceptions such as employees who have been with the company less than two years or who generally work fewer than 20 hours per week.

▪ You may have to pay AMT if you exercise an ISO and hold the shares after the end of the year. AMT does not apply to the benefit you obtain from a bargain purchase under an ESPP.

▪ On the other hand, an ISO offers the opportunity to convert your entire profit into long-term capital gain, while you may have to treat some of your profit from an ESPP as compensation income even if you hold the shares long enough to avoid a disqualifying disposition.

Typical terms

Qualified employee stock purchase plans are peculiar in that the way they are described in the tax law doesn't match the way most of these plans work. The tax law describes them as plans under which employees receive options. With a few tweaks here and there, an incentive stock option plan could be turned into an employee stock purchase plan.

One of those tweaks is a pretty major one, though. A qualified ESPP has to be made available to all full-time employees on the same basis. Most companies that adopt these plans are so large that it would be difficult to administer a plan where everyone in the company receives ISO-style options. So companies have developed a different way of implementing these plans. Instead of receiving an option, you're offered an opportunity to buy stock at a favorable price through payroll deduction. You can choose to participate or not, and the IRS treats this as an option that meets the requirements for an employee stock purchase plan.

The specifics of these plans vary from one company to the next. The following is an outline of terms that might be considered typical. It's important to check the terms of your own company's plan because those terms may differ in important ways from those described below.

- If you want to participate, you have to sign up by a particular date to have from 1% to 10% of your pay withheld to purchase company stock over a particular *offering period.*

- The money will accumulate for that period of time, and then be used to buy stock at a price equal to 85% of the *lower* of the stock value at the beginning of that period or the stock value at the end of that period. That means your worst case scenario is that the stock price stays the same or goes down, and you buy for 15% below the price at the end of the period. If you're lucky, the stock price goes up, and your bargain will be bigger. For example, if the stock price is $10 at the beginning of the offering period and $12 at the end, the purchase price will be $8.50, nearly a 30% discount from the $12 price at the time of the purchase. At some companies the purchase price is simply 85% of the stock value at the end of the offering period, regardless of whether the stock went up or down.

- You can back out of the purchase at any time until close to the end of the offering period. (The deadline might be ten days before the end of the offering period, for example, to give the company time to process the paperwork.) If you withdraw from the purchase, the company will refund to you the money that was withheld from your paychecks.

The company doesn't *have* to offer a 15% discount. It can offer a smaller discount or none at all. Notice that you can still come out way ahead without a discount. If the stock went from $10 to $12 as in the example above, you would be purchasing $12 stock at $10 because the stock price went up during the offering period. If the stock doesn't go up during the offering period and you want to back out of the purchase, you can do so. Be sure to check the plan for the withdrawal deadline. Your only downside if you participate and then withdraw is that you don't get interest on the money that was held in the plan. That's usually a small price to pay for the possibility of buying stock at a bargain price.

27

ESPP Taxes and Strategies

The tax rules are generally favorable, but they can be tricky.

THE TAX RULES FOR AN EMPLOYEE STOCK PURCHASE PLAN depend on whether it's a qualified or nonqualified plan. Qualified ESPPs, also called 423 plans, are more common, but the tax rules for nonqualified ESPPs are much simpler, so we'll deal with those first.

Nonqualified ESPP

The tax law doesn't provide any special treatment for nonqualified ESPPs, so we apply the general rules. If you pay full price for the shares, you're treated exactly the same as if you made a purchase in the stock market. You have nothing to report at the time of the purchase, and any profit or loss when you sell the shares will be capital gain or loss.

If the amount you pay for the shares is less than their value at the time of the purchase, the difference will be treated as compensation income. Assuming you're treated as an employee, this income will be added to the wages reported on Form W-2. In addition, the company is required to withhold on this income.

> Methods for handling the withholding requirement vary. The company may take the withholding in cash from a regular paycheck, or it may reduce the number of shares you acquire and use cash equal to the value of the shares that were deducted to cover your withholding requirement, among other possibilities.

Selling shares. Any profit or loss you have when selling these shares will be capital gain or loss, which may be short-term or long-term depending on how long you hold the shares. There's just one thing you have to watch out for: your basis for these shares includes not just the amount you paid for them but also the amount of compensation income, if any, reported in connection with the purchase. Don't forget to include this added amount of basis—and if basis for the sale was reported by a broker, don't assume the broker included it. Double check, because when you sell shares, an increase in basis reduces your tax.

> Remember, your basis includes your purchase price plus any income reported on the purchase, but does *not* include any amount you paid toward income tax withholding or Social Security or Medicare tax.

Buying in a qualified ESPP

The beauty of a qualified employee stock purchase plan is that you have nothing at all to report when you acquire the stock, even if you're buying at a discount. No income on your tax return, and no alternative minimum tax either. When it comes to tax treatment of a valuable benefit from your employer, that's about as good as it gets.

I suppose it could be even better. You might want to claim a deduction for the amount of your paycheck that's used to buy the stock. Sorry, but that's not possible. You have to pay tax on that amount, just as if you received it in your paycheck and then used it to buy stock.

Companies generally provide tax-related information about purchases made through a qualified ESPP by the end of January of the year after the purchase. Although you receive this document, called *Form 3922*, for the year of purchase, you don't actually use the information until the year you dispose of the shares. If you still own your ESPP stock, you don't have to do anything with this form other than file it in a place where you can find it later. You'll need this information when you sell.

At that time you'll face some quirky rules, which are explained below. You'll want to keep the following points in mind:

- You may have to report compensation income even if you sell at a loss.

- Postponing a sale until after you satisfy the special holding period doesn't turn all your profit into capital gain.

- Compensation income can be triggered by gifts or even a transfer at death.

Special holding period

Just like ISOs, employee stock purchase plans have a special holding period. The tax treatment of your sale will depend on whether you satisfied this test. You meet the holding period requirement on the *later* of the following two dates:

- The date two years after the company granted the option.

- The date one year after you received the stock.

Now we're back to talking about *options*. Under these plans you don't receive an option in the traditional sense, so when does the two-year period start to run? Regulations that came out in 2009 say the two-year holding period generally begins on the same day the offering period begins. (Remember that the *offering period* is the time during which the company is taking deductions from your pay.) Your company should notify you if special circumstances exist calling for the use of a different starting date.

The offering period is often six months, but it can be shorter or longer. If it's less than a year, you'll satisfy the special holding period if you hold the stock until after the second anniversary of the start of the offering period. If you receive your stock at least a year after the start of the offering period, the special holding period would be satisfied when you held the stock more than a year after receiving it.

> Any compensation income you have under the rules described below should be reported as wages on your tax return. Check to see if the company included this income on your W-2, and if not, simply add it to your W-2 income when you fill out your Form 1040.

Early disposition

If you sell the stock or otherwise dispose of it before satisfying the special holding period, you have an early disposition (or *disqualifying* disposition). In determining what events count as a disposition, the same rules that apply to stock from incentive stock options apply to stock from employee stock purchase plans. See Chapter 15 for details.

When you make an early disposition you have to report compensation income equal to the bargain element when you bought the stock—that is, at the end of the offering period. The *bargain element* is the difference between the value of the stock on that date and the amount you paid for it.

Example: The stock traded at $10 per share at the beginning of a six-month offering period and $11 at the end of that period, when the purchase occurred. The employee stock purchase plan offers a 15% discount from the lower of those values, so you buy the stock at $8.50 per share. If you sell the stock—or give it away—before satisfying the special holding period, you'll report $2.50 per share of compensation income. That's the difference between the $11 value and the $8.50 purchase price.

You have to report this amount of compensation income even if you don't have a profit on the sale of the stock. (That's a difference from incentive stock options, by the way.) The compensation income increases your basis in the stock, and reduces your capital gain (or increases your capital loss).

Example: In the example above you had to report $2.50 of compensation income. You paid $8.50 for the stock, and this $2.50 would increase your basis to $11 per share. If you sold the stock for $7, you would report a capital loss of $4 per share (in addition to reporting $2.50 of compensation income). If you used the stock to make a gift, you would still report $2.50 of income and the basis of the stock at the time of the gift would be $11 per share.

It's possible, of course, that you'll have a profit on your sale that's larger than the amount of compensation income you reported. In that situation you'll report capital gain in addition to compensation income. The capital gain will be long-term if you held the stock more than a year before the sale.

> You can hold the stock more than a year but still have an early disposition if you didn't satisfy the two-year rule. In that case you still report compensation income as described above but any capital gain or loss you have in addition is long-term.

Example: Same as the previous example, except you sold for $15 per share. Your basis, after adjusting for the $2.50 of compensation income, is $11 per share, so you report $4 per share of capital gain.

Holding period satisfied

Now things get interesting. You may still have to report compensation income if you sell *after* satisfying the special holding period (another difference from the rules for incentive stock options). The rule for determining *how much* compensation income to report is a little peculiar.

First, the good news. If you don't have any profit, you don't report any compensation income. That's a much better deal than when you make an early sale. As explained above, you have to report compensation income on an early sale, even if you sell at a loss.

If you sell at a profit, you have to report compensation income. The amount you report is the *lesser* of the amount of your profit or . . . or what? You're probably thinking it's the bargain element again—but it's not. Instead, it's the difference between the stock value *when the option was granted* (which generally means at the *beginning* of the offering period, not the *end*, when you bought the stock) and the *option price*, which for this purpose is *also* determined as of the beginning of the offering period.

Example: Let's stick with the example we've been using. The value of the stock at the beginning of the offering period is $10 per share, and you buy the stock for $8.50 per share at the end of that period when it's trading at $11. If you sell the stock at $14 after the end of the special holding period, you have to report compensation income equal to the difference between $10 and $8.50, or $1.50 per share. That's less than the $2.50 per share bargain element you would report if you sold before the end of the special holding period. You also report $4 per share of capital gain.

Another: Change the facts. At the end of the offering period the stock is down to $8 per share. The plan says you pay 85% of the *lower* of the price at the beginning of the offering period or the price at the end. That means you pay 85% of $8, or 6.80 per share. The stock's price recovers and you end up selling at $14. You still report compensation income of $1.50 per share, because the bargain element at the time of exercise doesn't matter. You would add $1.50 to your purchase price of $6.80 to come up with a basis of $8.30. Your capital gain on the sale would be $5.70.

If that gives you a headache, you're not alone. Many people get this rule wrong, including the plan administrators at some large companies. There's a worksheet in Chapter 30 that lays out the calculation in simplified form.

> When you buy stock at a discount through a qualified ESPP, you should receive Form 3922 from the company. This form provides much of the information needed to determine the amount of compensation income to report when you sell shares.

Pop quiz

Feeling smart? Try this one. In the last example above, other things being equal, should you sell before or after satisfying the special holding period? Did you come up with the surprising answer? You do better if you sell early. The amount of ordinary income on an early sale is $1.20, the amount of the bargain element at the end of the offering period. Once you satisfy the special holding period, you have to measure your compensation income as of the *beginning* of the offering period, when the spread was $1.50 per share. The total amount of income is the same in both cases, but an early sale lets you report more of your income as capital gain.

ESPP strategies

An ESPP can provide a welcome boost to your finances. Let's consider how you can best take advantage.

Buying shares. Should you participate? I would say yes. It makes sense to own at least some stock in the company where you work as a show of commitment and a way to participate in the success of a common effort. Personally, I would want to do this even if the company didn't offer an ESPP and I had use a regular brokerage account to buy shares.

Your purchase has to make sense as an investment, of course. Before you commit a substantial sum to purchase stock through an ESPP, consider your other priorities. Paying off high-interest debt from credit cards or other sources, or making full use of matching contributions available for 401k contributions, would likely rank higher than boosting your ESPP purchases, even if the plan offers a 15% discount.

You should also consider how a purchase of shares affects the overall balance of your portfolio. Generally it's unwise to have a large portion of your net worth tied to the value of a single stock. Yet the usual argument for diversification may not apply with quite the same force here. We saw in Chapter 5 that the added risk from failing to diversify is undesirable because it isn't compensated with an expectation of higher returns. When you buy shares at a discount through an ESPP, you're being compensated to take that risk.

All investments carry risk of loss, and you should be aware that the price of your company's stock may decline more than 15%, putting you in a losing position despite the discount. Yet the discount makes this opportunity highly favorable, provided that your overall financial condition permits you to bear this risk.

Selling shares. A sale of ESPP shares should be primarily an investment decision. You may have determined that your overall exposure to this particular stock is excessive, or simply decided you want to deploy the funds elsewhere, such as a down payment on a new home. Yet in some situations it pays to be aware of tax consequences, particularly if you're close to satisfying the holding period for a qualifying sale.

Example: Your company's stock took off during the offering period and you ended up buying $25,000 worth of stock for $10,000. Since then the stock price has settled back to $12,000 and now you're considering a sale. If this is a disqualifying disposition, you'll be required to report $15,000 of income. You'll also have a $13,000 capital loss, but unless you have capital gains from another source you'll deduct only $3,000 of your capital loss, and carry the rest to the following year. You end up paying tax on $12,000 of income even though your profit was only $2,000.

It's a different story if you sell after satisfying the special holding period. Now your compensation income is limited to the amount of your profit. You'll report just $2,000 of compensation income and zero capital gain or loss—a much better result.

Continuing to hold on exposes you to the risk of a further drop in the value of the stock, of course. You need to consider this risk as part of your decision whether to avoid the bad tax result of a disqualifying disposition.

Finally, it can be useful to keep in mind the little quirk that sometimes gives you a *better* result from a disqualifying disposition. This happens when the stock went *down* in value during the offering period but then went *up* in value before you sold it (see the "pop quiz" earlier). Even when this happens, an early sale may not save you any money because your capital gain may be taxed the same as ordinary income. If your gain is long-term, or if you have capital losses that can absorb the gain, you may benefit from selling before the stock matures.

Part IX
Other Topics

28

Private or Pre-IPO Companies

Equity compensation from companies that aren't publicly traded can raise special issues.

MUCH OF OUR DISCUSSION HAS PROCEEDED with the implicit or explicit assumption that your company's stock is publicly traded. Some companies prefer to remain privately held, while others intend to be publicly traded but are not yet ready for their initial public offering, or IPO. These companies are subject to the same tax rules that apply to publicly traded companies, but some of the planning considerations may be different.

Value of the stock

The value of publicly traded stock is generally the current price established by the stock market. Without this objective measure, we need another way to determine the value of stock in private companies. In most cases where a private company issues options, the board of directors (or a committee of the board) announces the value from time to time.

The most persuasive factor in valuing privately held stock is the price paid in recent arms-length sales. Yet pre-IPO companies often sell stock to venture capitalists and other investors under special terms that provide the purchaser with rights beyond those of ordinary shareholders. The "VCs" may receive preferred stock, or special voting rights, or representation on the board of directors, or all of the above. As a result, the price they pay for their shares may bear little relationship to the value of shares you can buy with your stock options. It isn't unusual for the announced price of common shares to be a small fraction of the price paid by venture capitalists in a recent round of financing.

The value of your company can depend on a variety of other factors, such as profits, cash flow, or net worth (assets minus debts and other liabilities). In some industries the value of a company may relate closely to a particular measure, such as the number and size of accounts or how many people visit the company's web site. Inevitably the value of a private company is somewhat subjective.

Value of your option

If the value of the stock is somewhat subjective, the value of your options is even more so. The Black-Scholes formula is useless without an indication of the stock's volatility. If the stock isn't publicly traded, we have no way of telling how much the value of the stock fluctuates from time to time.

> For some purposes the IRS may value an option on a privately held company by comparison to options to buy stock of a public company that's similar to the private company.

In most situations it's appropriate to treat pre-IPO stock as if it were highly volatile. That means the time value of the option may be unusually high. It also means there's a significant chance that you'll never reap any value at all from your option. Very often, options on pre-IPO stock are like lottery tickets, paying off at very high levels or not paying off at all.

High-risk stock compensation

I heard this story from a guy who received close to $500,000 worth of pre-IPO stock for his services as a non-employee consultant. He hoped the stock would be worth millions after the IPO, but the company failed to go public and the stock ended up being worthless. Because the stock was worth $500,000 when he received it, he owed about $200,000 of income tax and self-employment tax. This is a case where someone took a huge risk—a *tax* risk—even though he paid nothing at all for the stock.

Proper planning would have allowed him to avoid this situation. For example, instead of $500,000 worth of stock he could have accepted options worth $500,000. Delayed vesting is another approach that might work in a situation like this. Because of the risk the stock would be worthless, it was important to avoid owing tax now on its speculative value.

High-risk option exercise

When you exercise an option on pre-IPO stock, you take economic risk in addition to tax risk. No matter how good the company's prospects seem, there's no way to be sure an IPO will be successful until it actually happens. When you exercise an option prior to an IPO you should take into account the very real possibility that your stock will turn out to be worthless. In that event you can be stuck with the tax consequences of exercising the option and the loss of any funds used to exercise the option.

Compare those risks with the potential payoff from exercising your option after the IPO. On a pre-tax basis you're in the same position either way. There may be a significant tax benefit in exercising earlier, however.

Example: You have an option to buy 10,000 shares of pre-IPO stock at $1 per share. The current value of the stock is $2 per share. You believe a successful IPO is likely, and will leave you with stock worth $20 per share. If you exercise the option after the IPO, you'll have to report $190,000 of compensation income (the $200,000 value reduced by the $10,000 purchase price).

If instead you exercise the option now, you'll report only $10,000 of compensation income. Later you'll report $180,000 of long-term capital gain on a sale of the stock for $200,000. Overall, you may have reduced your federal income tax on this profit by $35,000.

Well, $35,000 is a nice chunk of change, but you're taking a lot more risk to get there. If the IPO doesn't come off, your stock may turn out to be worthless. You'll have lost the $10,000 you paid to exercise the option, and you'll be out thousands more because you had to pay tax on the compensation income you reported when you exercised the option. You'll also have a potential tax benefit from a $20,000 capital loss on the sale or worthlessness of your shares, but you may not get full benefit for that loss because of the $3,000 capital loss limitation.

There's no rule of thumb that tells you when the risk is worth taking. It's a judgment call based on the tax consequences and whatever can be discerned about the company's prospects.

Fair Market Value

Your tax consequences can depend on the fair market value
of the shares you acquire from your company.

WHEN YOU REPORT COMPENSATION INCOME from stock or
options, the amount of income will be measured by the *fair market
value* of the stock. There's a classical definition of this term that
many tax professionals know by heart:

> Fair market value is the price at which the property would change
> hands between a willing buyer and a willing seller, neither being
> under any compulsion to buy or to sell and both having reasonable
> knowledge of relevant facts.

This definition takes you a good part of the way toward understanding the concept. See Chapter 28 for additional thoughts on
valuing stock in private or pre-IPO companies. In this chapter we'll
expand on the subject under the following headings:

- Valuing publicly traded stock
- How restrictions affect value
- Discounts

Valuing publicly traded stock

Stock is publicly traded if you can buy or sell it on an established securities market, or through some other system that acts as the equivalent of a securities market. In general the stock market determines the value of publicly traded stock. The usual rule is that the value on any given day is the average of the high and low selling prices on that day, although the previous day's closing price may be used for some purposes.

Employers sometimes use variations on this rule. If the stock is very thinly traded, it may make sense to use an average over a period of several trading days so that a single transaction won't have undue effect on the value. There isn't any regulation that permits this approach, but we don't see the IRS challenging reasonable variations unless they provide opportunities for manipulation.

It's somewhat unusual, but not impossible, for publicly traded stock to qualify for a blockage discount as explained below.

Effect of restrictions

You may feel that restrictions on the stock you acquired make it less valuable than it would otherwise be. But there's a special rule here: when you determine the value of your shares, you have to ignore all restrictions except those that are permanent. If your stock is restricted for a limited period of time, or until some event occurs, you have to ignore the restriction when you determine the value of the stock.

Certain permanent restrictions count in determining value, however. If your stock is subject to a permanent restriction, review the discussion of *non-lapse restrictions* in Chapter 22. You may be able to take that restriction into account in determining the value of the stock.

Discounts

There are circumstances that can justify a discount in the value of your stock. One recognized discount applies when there's no market for the stock: a discount for *lack of marketability*. Another discount can apply where there's a market for the stock, but the size of your holdings is large enough to make efficient sale impossible: a *blockage* discount. The availability of these discounts, and the appropriate size of the discount, should be determined by a qualified appraiser or tax professional.

30

Income Tax Reporting

Reporting for equity compensation can be confusing, even
for tax professionals.

THIS BOOK LAYS OUT NUMEROUS SPECIAL TAX RULES that
apply to equity compensation. It's one thing to understand the rules
and use them in planning. Translating those rules into an accurately
prepared income tax return is a distinct challenge. The guidance that
follows is not intended to be comprehensive, but should get you
pointed in the right direction. This chapter assumes you're an
employee (that is, someone who receives Form W-2), and is based
on IRS forms that were used for tax returns filed in 2013.

> Generally you have to be concerned with two transactions: one in
> which you acquire the shares, and one in which you sell them. Even
> if you sell the shares at the same time you acquire them, your tax
> return will have to reflect two distinct events.

Restricted stock units

If you receive a restricted stock unit, stock is not transferred to you until you've satisfied the vesting condition. The value of the stock as of that date is treated as compensation income. You don't have to do anything special to report this income because it will be included, along with your other wages, in box 1 of Form W-2. Simply report that figure as wages, the way you normally would, and you will have satisfied your obligation to report this income.

You must, however, make note of *how much* income was reported, because this is your *basis* for the shares, used in determining how much gain or loss you'll report when you sell the shares. This figure may appear in box 14 of Form W-2. If not, track it down through whatever other documentation you received from the company in connection with the transfer. Note also the date of the transfer, as this will determine whether gain or loss in a subsequent sale is short-term or long-term.

No special tax treatment applies to sales of RSU stock. You're treated the same as if you had received cash compensation and used it to invest in the stock. Check carefully, however, to make sure the basis is correctly reported.

Restricted stock grants, vested

If stock you receive due to a restricted stock grant is vested when you receive it, the tax treatment is the same as described above for RSUs. Income will appear as part of your wages on Form W-2, and this income will establish your basis for the shares.

Restricted stock grants, 83b election

If stock you receive due to a restricted stock grant is *not* vested when you receive it, you may choose to file the 83b election. In this case the shares will be treated as if they were vested when you received them and your tax treatment will be the same as described earlier for vested shares, with the following caveats:

- The 83b election is not valid unless filed within 30 days after you receive the stock.

- You're required to attach a copy of the 83b election to your income tax return for the year you received the stock.

- Income you report as a result of making this election becomes your basis for the shares, used to determine gain or loss in a later sale, but if you subsequently forfeit the shares, you can't claim a loss. You report nothing at all in connection with a forfeiture.

Restricted stock grants, not vested

If the stock is not vested and you don't file the 83b election, you have nothing to report in connection with the transfer of the shares to you. Instead, you will report compensation income when the shares vest, based on the value of the shares at that time. Your tax treatment will be the same as if you vested in an RSU on that date (see above). Note that for purposes of determining whether your capital gain on a subsequent sale is short-term or long-term, your holding period for these shares begin on the vesting date, not on the date they were originally transferred to you.

Nonqualified stock option

Shares received upon exercise of a nonqualified stock option are normally vested. In this case you will report compensation income equal to the difference between the value of the shares when you exercised the option and the exercise price of the option. This income will appear, together with other wage income, in box 1 of Form W-2. It should also be broken out as a separate number in box 12, designated with code V. *Do not add this amount to the wages in box 1, because it's already included in that number.*

247

You'll need this number, however, when you sell the shares. Your basis for the shares is the exercise price of the option increased by the amount of income reported in connection with the exercise. These two numbers added together should equal the value of the shares as of the date of exercise. Note that your basis *does not* include any tax withholding you were required to pay when you exercised the option. Apart from the need to make this basis adjustment, no special tax treatment is required for a sale of these shares.

> Basis reported by a broker for sale of these shares may or may not include this basis adjustment. See *Reporting Stock Sales*, below.

ISO Form 3921

Each year you exercise an incentive stock option you should receive, in addition to Form W-2 (and about the same time), Form 3921, providing vital tax information relating to your option exercise:

- The date the option was granted
- The date it was exercised
- The exercise price
- The value on the exercise date

This information is required in determining whether you've made a disqualifying disposition, the amount of compensation income (if any) you need to report, and your tax consequences under the alternative minimum tax (AMT).

ISO same-year sale

Reporting for incentive stock options can be complicated, but it's relatively simple when you sell the shares the same year you exercise the option. You'll have two different items to report: compensation income from exercise of the option, and capital gain or loss on sale of the stock. That's true even if you arranged to have these two events occur simultaneously.

Compensation income. When you sell ISO shares the same year you exercise the option, you've made a disqualifying disposition. In certain types of transactions (see *Other Early Dispositions* in Chapter 15) you have to report compensation income equal to the full bargain element when you exercised the option. When the sale is made to an unrelated person without a purchase of replacement shares, however, compensation income is limited to your actual profit.

This compensation income *may or may not* be included with other income in box 1 of Form W-2. It will not be broken out in box 12, but may appear in box 14 or supplementary information provided by your employer. In a pinch, you may be able to determine how much was treated this way on Form W-2 by comparing total wages in box 1 with Medicare wages in box 5. Compensation from a disqualifying disposition of ISO stock is not included in Medicare wages.

If the proper amount is included in the figure appearing in box 1, you'll simply report that number as usual. If this amount is not included, you still have to report it as wages. Add it to the amount appearing in box 1 when entering the amount of wages on your income tax return. Attach a statement indicating the amount added and the reason.

Sale of shares. Report the sale as you would any other sale of stock, making sure you include in your basis the compensation income reported in connection with the disqualifying disposition. See *Reporting Stock Sales,* below. Note that if you're selling at a price between the exercise price of the option and the fair market value as of the date of exercise, this sale will produce zero gain or loss, because the amount of compensation income reported will be equal to the amount required to make your basis match the selling price.

AMT. When you sell ISO stock the same year you exercised the option, you have nothing to report on the AMT form for either the purchase or the sale.

ISO exercise without sale

Things get interesting when you exercise an incentive stock option and hold the stock after the end of the year. For the year of exercise, your regular income tax is not affected, but you'll have to report an "AMT adjustment" equal to the bargain element on line 14 of Form 6251, the form used to calculate alternative minimum tax. If you received Form 3921 from the company, you should find the information required to calculate this adjustment on that form. Otherwise you'll have to obtain that information elsewhere.

> **Example:** Form 3921 says you paid $18 per share to acquire stock with a value of $35 per share, and the number of shares is 200. You'll report $3,400 (200 x $17, the difference between $35 and $18) on line 14 of Form 6251.

Forms required in subsequent years

If you paid AMT (or *increased* AMT) as a result of exercising an ISO in a prior year, you'll have three possibilities for any subsequent year:

- You sold shares in a disqualifying disposition.
- You sold shares after meeting the special holding period.
- You didn't sell any shares, either because you continue to hold shares or because you sold them all in a previous year.

In all three cases you have to file Form 6251 (the AMT form) and Form 8801 (used to claim AMT credit) until you no longer have any unused AMT credit. Do this every year, even if you haven't sold any of your shares—and even after you've sold all of them—until the credit disappears.

ISO qualifying sale

When you sell ISO stock that's been held long enough to avoid a disqualifying disposition, you have to report the sale for both regular income tax and AMT purposes. Your gain or loss won't be the same in both calculations because your AMT basis for the stock includes the bargain element that you reported as AMT income for the year you exercised the option.

Regular tax gain or loss. Report gain or loss as you would for any sale of stock. Your basis is simply the amount you paid to exercise the option.

AMT gain or loss. You will need to fill out an AMT version of Form 8949 and Schedule D. These are not to be filed with your return, but are used to determine the amount of AMT adjustment due to the sale.

> **Example:** You paid $20,000 for stock valued at $50,000. After satisfying the ISO holding period, you sold the stock for $60,000.

For regular income tax purposes you have a capital gain of $40,000 (difference between the $60,000 selling price and the amount you paid for the stock). For AMT purposes your basis includes the $30,000 of income included on your AMT form for the year of exercise, so you have AMT capital gain of $10,000.

If these are your only items of capital gain or loss, the result will be an overall difference of $30,000 between the regular tax Schedule D and the AMT Schedule D. Other items of gain or loss, together with the $3,000 capital loss limitation, could affect the result, however.

> **Example:** Continuing the previous example, suppose you also have a capital loss of $22,000 from an unrelated source.

On Schedule D as prepared for regular income tax you can fully use this loss because you have capital gain of $40,000 from selling your

ISO stock. On the AMT version of Schedule D, you have only $10,000 of gain from selling your ISO stock. When combined with the unrelated $22,000 loss, the overall result is a $12,000 loss, but the $3,000 capital loss limitation applies. You would have $18,000 of capital gain for regular income tax purposes and $3,000 of capital loss for AMT purposes, for an overall difference of $21,000. You would also have a $9,000 capital loss carryover—but only for AMT purposes.

AMT adjustment. The difference between gain or loss for regular tax purposes and for AMT purposes must be reported on Form 6251. It goes on line 17 as a negative number. This number is negative because it is a *favorable* AMT adjustment, one that either reduces the amount of AMT you pay or increases the amount of AMT credit you can claim. *Don't make the mistake of reporting this adjustment as a positive number!*

Reminder. You will also have to file Form 8801 for this year, unless you somehow consumed your entire AMT credit before selling these shares.

ISO disqualifying sale in later year

We covered a same-year sale of ISO stock earlier. It's also possible to have a disqualifying disposition in a subsequent year.

> **Example:** You exercised an ISO in November and sold shares the following March. This is a disqualifying disposition because you didn't hold the shares at least a year after exercising the option.

Tax reporting for this type of sale is a little tricky.

Compensation income. For purposes of the regular income tax you'll report compensation income as discussed earlier (see *ISO Same-Year Sale*). This compensation income may or may not be reflected in your Form W-2.

AMT adjustment. This is where you have to be careful. We saw earlier that you don't need an AMT adjustment when you make a same-year sale, because your income and basis are the same for AMT purposes as for regular income tax purposes. That's not true when your disqualifying sale occurs after the end of the year you exercised the option. For AMT purposes, you already reported compensation income in the year you exercised the option. Your AMT adjustment in the year of sale has to accomplish two things: (1) eliminate the compensation income you're reporting for regular income tax purposes, and (2) adjust the basis of the shares to reflect the income reported for AMT purposes when you exercised the option.

Example: You exercised an ISO in November, paying $20,000 to buy stock worth $80,000 on the date of exercise. Six months later you sold the stock for $65,000.

For the year of exercise you reported $60,000 of compensation income solely for AMT purposes. For the year you sold the stock, your regular income tax reflects $45,000 of compensation income and zero capital gain or loss (because your basis includes the amount paid to exercise the option plus the compensation income). For AMT purposes you need an adjustment that eliminates the $45,000 of income. You also need an adjustment in capital gain or loss, because your basis for AMT purposes is $80,000 ($20,000 purchase price plus $60,000 of compensation income reported for the year of exercise). As discussed earlier, this adjustment can be affected by other capital gains and losses unrelated to sales of ISO stock. In this example, if you have no other capital gains or losses, your AMT result would be a capital loss of $15,000. You're allowed to deduct only $3,000 this year (the rest carries over to the following year), so your total AMT adjustment is $48,000: $45,000 to eliminate the compensation income and $3,000 to reflect the difference in capital gain or loss.

These adjustments are combined and reported on line 17 of Form 6251. Although they're reported together on the same line, the portion of the adjustment that relates to capital gain or loss can have a different effect than the part that relates to compensation income because of the special tax rates that apply to long-term capital gain.

> A comprehensive example of these adjustments appears in the IRS instructions for Form 6251.

Nonqualified ESPP

A purchase of stock through a nonqualified ESPP, and a subsequent sale of the shares, are reported the same as if you acquired the shares by exercising a nonqualified stock option, as described earlier.

ESPP Form 3922

Each year you buy stock through a qualified employee stock purchase plan, you should receive Form 3922 about the same time you receive Form W-2. (For technical reasons, some companies may not provide this form until the year you sell or otherwise dispose of your shares.) You'll need the information in this form when you sell your shares, even if you make a qualifying sale years later, so make it part of your permanent records.

ESPP purchase

You report nothing at all upon a purchase of shares through a qualified ESPP. If you received Form 3922 but you haven't sold the shares, simply hold onto that form. Nothing goes on your tax return for the year of purchase.

ESPP disqualifying disposition

Selling shares before you satisfy the special holding period is a disqualifying disposition. The tax treatment is the same whether this happens the same year you bought the shares or a later year.

Compensation income. You'll report compensation income equal to the difference between the value of the shares when you bought them and the amount you paid for the stock. This income is *not* limited to the amount of actual profit you have on the sale, so you could have a situation where you report compensation income on the sale even if you lost money. The income may or may not be included with other compensation in the amount reported as wages on Form W-2. If it's included there, simply report your W-2 wages as usual; if not, add this income to the amount you report as wages on your tax return.

Sale of stock. You'll also have to report the sale of the stock, which will result in a capital gain or loss. Be sure to adjust your basis to include the amount of compensation income reported as described in the previous paragraph.

ESPP qualifying sale

Unlike an ISO, an ESPP does not always eliminate the need to report compensation income if you hold the shares long enough to avoid a disqualifying disposition. If you have to report income, check to see whether it's already included on your Form W-2.

The rule for determining the amount of income to report in this case is tricky, and we've seen many mistakes by taxpayers, tax professionals, and in some cases, the companies that run these plans. In the following worksheet, the "as if" stock price is the amount you would have paid if you bought the stock at the beginning of the offering period. If you have Form 3922 for these shares, this is the number in box 8 on that form.

ESPP Holding Period Satisfied (Qualifying Disposition)

1   Stock value at beginning of offering period   _____

2   "As if" stock price (see explanation above)   _____

3   Line 1 minus line 2   _____

4   Sale proceeds or value on date of disposition   _____

5   Amount paid for stock   _____

6   Line 4 minus line 5 but not less than zero   _____

7   Compensation (lesser of line 3 or line 6)   _____

Sale of stock. Here again you have to report the sale of the shares, taking care to increase your basis to reflect the amount of compensation income reported in connection with the sale.

Reporting sales of stock

We used to report sales of stock on Schedule D. Now they go on Form 8949, with the results summarized on Schedule D.

One reason for this change is that brokers are now required to report the basis of shares in many sale transactions, but not all. The IRS wants you to separate the sales for which basis was reported from the ones for which basis was not reported. If you have some in each category, you'll report them on separate Forms 8949. Here are the key points to remember.

Basis reported or not. Carefully review Form 1099-B and any other tax information you received from the broker to determine whether basis information was reported to the IRS. In some cases the broker may provide basis information for your convenience even when the broker is not reporting this information to the IRS, so read carefully to determine which category applies.

Basis not reported. When basis is not reported by the broker, you'll have to determine basis from other records. Generally your basis will be the amount (if any) you paid for the shares, plus the amount (if any) of compensation income reported on the shares (either when you received them or when you sold them). It's a good idea to cross check the amount of compensation income included in your basis against the amount that was reported as wages in connection with these shares.

Broker reports basis. You may receive information from the broker indicating that basis was reported to the IRS. For technical reasons, the basis reported by the broker may or may not include an adjustment for the amount of compensation income you reported on the shares. *Don't assume that the basis reported by the broker is correct!* Calculate the basis from other records, just as you would if the broker had not reported basis.

If the basis reported by the broker is correct, you're good to go. If not, you'll have to report an adjustment when you fill out Form 8949. You don't have to contact the broker for a corrected Form 1099-B. The IRS understands that many taxpayers will have to make adjustments of this kind. Check the IRS instructions for Form 8949. Note that you're making an adjustment to gain or loss, *not* an adjustment to basis. An increase in basis (for example, to reflect compensation income the broker didn't take into account) is a *decrease* in gain or loss, so this adjustment would appear as a negative number (that is, in parentheses). Code B is used to indicate that the broker reported incorrect basis.

It's a good idea to attach a statement explaining the adjustment, such as "broker's reported basis did not include adjustment for compensation income reported on exercise of option."

31

Estimated Tax Payments

If withholding doesn't cover your income tax, you may have to make estimated tax payments.

IF YOU'RE AN EMPLOYEE, you may have never had to worry about making estimated tax payments. The amount of income tax withheld from paychecks may be enough to cover the tax you owe and then some, providing a refund. Even if you owe some tax on April 15, estimates aren't required unless you owe more than $1,000.

When you receive compensation in stock and options, there's a good chance you'll end up with a tax bill of more than $1,000 at some point. In that situation, it's possible that you'll incur a penalty if you don't make quarterly payments of estimated tax.

First things you should know

If you've never had to deal with estimated taxes before, the whole idea can seem foreign and uncomfortable. There are two things you should know right away to put your mind at rest.

- **It's easy.** In most cases, the process of figuring out how much to pay isn't hard at all. And paying the tax is a snap.

- **No jail time.** You won't go to jail if you make a mistake and pay too little. In fact, the penalty isn't exactly a killer. It's just simple interest on the amount you underpaid, and the interest rate isn't terribly high. If you somehow blow it and underpay by $400, and correct the underpayment with your next payment three months later, your penalty might be about $10. It's better to avoid the penalty, but really, this is nothing to lose sleep over.

General rule: 90%

The general rule is that your estimated tax payments, when added to your withholding and credits, must add up to 90% of the current year's tax liability. If your withholding and credits already add up to 90% of your tax liability, you don't have to make estimated tax payments. Yet in many cases you don't have to make estimated tax payments even if your withholding and credits fall short of the 90% figure, for reasons described below.

> When we talk about the *tax due,* we mean the total amount of tax you owe—including any self-employment tax and the dreaded alternative minimum tax (AMT).

Tax due less than $1,000

Here's a rule that makes it easy for many people who have withholding that falls just a bit short to avoid dealing with estimated tax payments. No payment is required if the amount due after subtracting withholding and credits will be less than $1,000.

Example: Suppose you expect your wage withholding to be just enough to cover your income tax liability. Then you have a long-term capital gain you didn't plan on, and the added tax is $600. You can make an estimated tax payment if you feel more comfortable doing so, but there won't be a penalty if you wait until April 15 of next year to send in the payment because it's less than $1,000.

The only problem with this rule is that sometimes it's difficult to know what your tax liability will be. But $1,000 is a reasonable amount of leeway for the majority of taxpayers.

Prior year safe harbor

Most people can avoid paying estimated tax if their withholding and credits equal 100% of the tax shown on the *prior year's* income tax return. I call this the *prior year safe harbor.*

There's a related rule. You don't have to pay estimated tax if all of the following are true:

- You had no tax liability for the previous year.
- You were a U.S. citizen or resident for the entire year.
- Your tax year covered a 12-month period.

The prior year safe harbor often permits taxpayers to avoid making estimated payments if they receive a large sum of income on a one-time basis.

> **Example:** In a normal year withholding is enough to cover your income tax—in fact, you usually get a small refund. This year you exercise an incentive stock option and then sell the stock. As a result, you report $200,000 of income. Despite this huge increase in income, you don't have to make estimated tax payments if your withholding will be at least equal to the tax shown on the prior year's tax return.

Higher income, higher percentage. There's a rule that requires taxpayers with adjusted gross income above $150,000 on the prior year's return ($75,000 if married filing separately) to pay 110% of the prior year's tax (not just 100%) when applying the prior year safe harbor. Congress has been known to tinker with this percentage, so check the form instructions.

Even if the prior year safe harbor doesn't allow you to completely avoid making estimated tax payments, it permits you to determine an amount that will avoid a penalty without making an accurate estimate of the current year's taxes.

Example: Your income tax for last year was $24,000. You expect your withholding for this year to be $21,000. You don't know how much income you'll have for this year, though, because you may sell stock at a gain. Because of the prior year safe harbor, you can safely cover your estimated tax requirement by paying $3,000 ($750 per quarter). When added to your $21,000 of withholding, you'll have total payments that equal your prior year's tax.

There are situations where it doesn't make sense to use the prior year safe harbor. You may have a year in which you had an unusually large amount of income. When the next year rolls around, you would be paying estimates that are larger than necessary if you pay based on that banner year. In this case you'll want to estimate the current year's tax and try to pay at least 90% of that number.

Example: Last year you exercised nonqualified options and reported an extra $80,000 of income. This year you won't have that extra income, but still need to make estimated tax payments. If you base the payment amount on your tax for last year, you'll pay $30,000 more than necessary. It makes more sense to use a realistic estimate of this year's tax.

Estimating your tax

As you've seen above, there are plenty of situations where it isn't actually necessary to do any estimating when you make estimated tax payments. But sometimes you need to make an estimate of the current year's tax. Otherwise you'll either pay way too much, or come up short and end up with a penalty.

Form 1040-ES (the form used to pay estimated tax) comes with a worksheet you can use to estimate how much tax you'll owe for the current year. There's certainly nothing wrong with using this worksheet—but most people don't. The reason is that the worksheet takes you through more detail than may be necessary, but still leaves you with nothing better than an educated guess about your tax liability. You don't file the worksheet with the IRS, and there's no requirement to justify how you came up with the amount of your estimated tax payment. So most people use a somewhat simplified method to figure their estimated tax:

- Look at each number on the prior year's tax return and ask yourself if this year's number is likely to be significantly different. Ignore differences in wages because there will be a corresponding difference in withholding. Use rounded numbers and don't worry about minor changes.

- Add up all the differences to see how much larger or smaller your taxable income will be for the current year.

- Apply the tax rates to see how much difference this will make in your income tax. (If the difference results from a long-term capital gain, apply the capital gain tax rates.) Round the number up or simply tack on an added amount if you want to increase your comfort level about avoiding a penalty.

Many people using this method don't bother looking up changes in the tax schedules that result from inflation adjustments. These changes will decrease your tax slightly, so that's one way of providing a cushion of extra payments. When there's a change in the tax rates or other important rules, though, as happened in 2013, check to see how they affect your tax.

Voluntary payments

Depending on your situation, the amount of estimated tax you're *required* to pay could be quite a bit less than your true estimate of the amount of tax you'll owe. That's because you're allowed to pay estimates based on the previous year's tax, even if you know this year's tax will be higher. When that happens you have a choice. You can pay the minimum amount required—and pay the rest on April 15. Or you can pay something close to the true estimate so you won't owe a lot on April 15. Which is better depends on your comfort level and money management skills.

Pay now and relax. Some people choose to make estimated payments even when the payments aren't required. The reason? Perhaps they're concerned that the money won't be there when they need it to pay taxes. Perhaps they're simply more comfortable knowing that they won't have a huge tax bill in April. There are a variety of good reasons to make estimated tax payments even if the payments aren't legally required. The biggest one is peace of mind.

Pay later and earn. The main reason *not* to pay more than you have to is that you lose the use of your money between the time you pay the estimate and the time you would have sent payment with your return. You should be able to earn at least a little bit of interest during that time. So there's at least one good reason to pay later, even though there are good reasons to pay sooner.

> If you take this approach, *don't get greedy*. Money you need for a tax payment next April should be invested conservatively to eliminate risk of loss.

Which is better. Which approach is better—making voluntary payments, or paying the minimum—depends on your personality and your circumstances. Consider the following example:

> **Example:** You normally don't pay estimates because your income is mainly from wages subject to withholding. In January this year you sell stock and have a capital gain of $30,000. You expect to owe $6,000 of tax, but you don't have to pay estimates because your withholding will be at least equal to your previous year's tax.

You have several choices, including the following:

- You can put $6,000 aside in an interest bearing account until April 15 of next year when the tax is due. This way you can make a little profit on the money before sending it to the IRS. If you have the discipline to leave the money alone, you come out ahead using this approach. There's a danger, though. If you start with this intention, but end up spending the money on a trip to Aruba, or losing it in a high-risk investment, you may wake up with a headache on April 15.

- You can send in a single estimated payment of $6,000. This approach is easy, and may seem relatively painless if you do it at a time when you're flush with money from the stock sale. It's also very safe: this approach assures that you won't somehow lose or spend the money before you file your tax return. It doesn't allow you to earn interest on the $6,000, though.

- You can send in four quarterly estimates of $1,500 each. You may prefer this approach if you don't like the idea of writing a single check for $6,000 to the IRS (who does?). And this approach gives you the flexibility to reduce later payments if you have a capital loss or other reduction in taxable income later in the year. There's a little more paperwork involved in this approach though, and more opportunity to lose or spend the money before you file your return.

There's nothing illegal or immoral about any of these approaches. They're all equally acceptable to the IRS. (They won't be upset if they receive a $6,000 payment for one quarter and no payment in later quarters.) If you find yourself in a situation like this, choose the approach that works best for you.

Increasing your withholding

There's a way you may be able to cover your extra tax liability without making estimated tax payments: increase the amount of tax withheld from your paycheck. You get a special benefit with this approach: extra withholding that comes late in the year is treated the same as if it was spread evenly over the year. You can use this approach to avoid late payment penalties.

How to do it. To increase the amount of federal income tax withheld from your paycheck, ask your employer for a new Form W-4. You're required to fill out this form when you start working for an employer. You can fill out a new one whenever your circumstances call for a change in the amount of withholding.

This form contains several worksheets, and the instructions tell you to "complete all worksheets that apply." But the worksheets are there mainly to make sure you don't *reduce* your withholding more than you're supposed to. There's never a problem when you want to *increase* your withholding. You can fill out the worksheets if you want, but you're not required to do so. And there's no particular need if the only thing you're doing is increasing your withholding to cover tax on your equity compensation.

There are two ways to increase your withholding on this form. One is to reduce the number of allowances you claim on the form. This can be a little tricky, because you don't necessarily know how much your withholding will change when you change your allowances. The amount depends on your income level and the withholding method adopted by your employer.

Some people are confused by *allowances*. You get one allowance for each exemption you can claim on your tax return (yourself, your spouse and your dependents), but an allowance isn't the same as an exemption. There are allowances for other items, such as deductions and certain credits. Reducing your allowances doesn't mean you'll claim fewer exemptions when you file your tax return. The number of allowances is used *only* to determine how much tax is withheld from your paycheck.

There's another approach that's simpler: request an "additional amount" to be withheld from your paycheck. Do this on line 6 of the form. This makes it fairly easy to determine the amount of the increase when you file Form W-4.

Check with your employer to find out when the change will go into effect. Normally there's a time lag between the day you fill out this form and the day it's processed, so you may not see the change in your very next paycheck. Keep an eye on your paycheck stubs to confirm that the change was properly made, and had the effect you anticipated.

Avoiding late payment penalty. The nice thing about using withholding to cover your estimated tax liability is that it can get you out of a late payment penalty. Withholding is presumed to be received evenly throughout the year.

Example: Suppose you realize in May that you need to pay $6,000 estimated tax for the year, and you've already blown the first $1,500 payment that was due April 15. It won't be a big deal if you send in the payment a few weeks late because the penalty isn't all that terrible. But you can avoid the penalty altogether by increasing your withholding for the rest of the year by $6,000. The IRS will treat the withholding as if it occurred evenly throughout the year, with $1,500 coming in the first quarter. You get the benefit of this assumption even if all of the added withholding comes in December!

Making estimated payments

Estimated payments for any year are due on April 15, June 15 and September 15 of that year, and January 15 of the following year. Whenever one of these dates falls on a legal holiday or on a weekend, the due date is the next day that isn't a holiday or weekend day. Here are some points to keep in mind:

- If you owe money with your tax return, *and* have to make an estimated tax payment, you have *two* checks to write on April 15. Be prepared!

- Although the payments are "quarterly," they aren't three months apart. The second payment sneaks up on you, just two months after the first one.

- Like your tax return, estimated payments are considered "on time" if you *mail* them by the due date.

- Most states that have an income tax require estimated payments on the same schedule as the federal payments. If you itemize deductions, it may be to your advantage to make your fourth quarter state estimated tax payment in December, not January, so you can deduct it a year earlier.

- A small number of individual taxpayers use a fiscal tax year that ends with a month other than December. Their payment schedule is different (but equivalent): the fifteenth day of the fourth, sixth and ninth months of their fiscal year, and the fifteenth day of the first month of the following fiscal year.

What to file. When you make estimated tax payments you need to enclose Form 1040-ES, Estimated Tax Voucher. This form is about as simple as they get. It asks for your name, address and social security number—and just one other item: the amount you're paying.

If you've previously made estimated tax payments, the IRS will send forms with your name, address and social security number pre-printed. Even if this is your first year paying estimates, the IRS will send pre-printed forms after they receive your first payment. You're not *required* to use these forms—don't panic if you lose them—but the IRS *prefers* that you use them to help assure that your payment will be processed promptly and correctly.

Form 1040-ES comes from the IRS as part of an intimidating package that includes lengthy instructions and detailed worksheets. As mentioned earlier, you don't have to fill out the worksheets unless you think they'll be helpful. And you should *never* send these worksheets to the IRS.

You can pay online. This is the preferred method, with least chance for something to go wrong. Visit irs.gov and look for a link that says "Pay your tax bill" or something similar. They offer various options, including electronic funds transfer or debit or credit card.

If paying by mail. *Estimated tax payments don't go to the same address as your return!* Don't enclose an estimated tax payment with your Form 1040. Check the instructions for Form 1040-ES for the proper address.

Enclose your check. Write your social security number on the check and a notation of what it's for, like this: 2007 2Q Form 1040-ES (assuming it's for the second quarter of 2007). If you're doing this before your first cup of coffee in the morning, double check to see that you *signed* the check.

Additional tips. You don't have to justify your estimated tax payments. In fact, there's no place for a *signature* on the form. When you send it in, you're not promising that this is the correct amount. All you're saying is, "Here's a payment to be applied toward my taxes."

Be sure to keep an accurate record of your estimated tax payments so you can claim credit for them when you file your return.

Joint payments. If you're married, you can make joint estimated tax payments with your spouse. (There's an exception if either spouse is a nonresident alien.) Paying joint estimated payments does *not* mean you have to file a joint return. But if you end up filing separately, you'll have to sort out who gets credit for what amount.

32

Protecting Gains Without Selling

There are ways to protect gains without selling shares, but usually it's better to sell, even if that means paying some tax.

WHEN YOUR STOCK OR OPTIONS BECOME VERY VALUABLE, it makes sense to think about protecting your gains. Normally the simplest way to do this is to cash out: exercise the options and sell the stock. You may be reluctant to take this action because of the tax consequences, or because it means giving up the remaining time value of your options, or perhaps simply out of a concern that the stock price will surge upward shortly after you sell, something that *always* seems to happen.

This chapter discusses some of the ways you may be able to protect yourself against a loss *without* cashing out your stock or options. These techniques have a number of drawbacks. They involve tax complexities—and tax risks—that can make them unattractive. They are often laden with costs that reduce their effectiveness, and some of these costs may be hidden.

Furthermore, most companies have policies against using these techniques. These policies usually don't appear as part of the stock option plan or agreement, but instead are stated as part of the company's policy on insider trading. Yet these policies apply more broadly than you might suppose: they may apply to all employees, not just top executives, and they aren't limited to situations where you're acting on the basis of inside information. A general policy against employees taking a short position in the company's stock or trading in options or other derivatives based on its stock is common. Depending on your company's view of these techniques, the policy may "strongly discourage" such transactions, or it may require advance permission, or it may prohibit them outright. Violations may result in sanctions, including termination of employment.

> Don't use the techniques described in this chapter unless you've confirmed that you can do so without violating your company's insider trading policy.

Short sales

One way to protect a built-in gain is through a *short sale*. When you sell short, some or all of the loss you have from a decline in the value of your stock or options will cancel out. This technique provides limited tax benefits, however:

- A short sale is treated as a disqualifying disposition of immature ISO stock or ESPP stock.

- A short sale prevents your stock from "aging" for purposes of getting long-term capital gain when you sell it.

- A short sale may be treated as a *constructive sale* in the year of the short sale, rather than in a later year when you dispose of your stock.

How a short sale works. A short sale is a transaction in which you sell stock that's owned by someone else. If you tell your broker to sell 100 shares of XYZ short, your broker will *borrow* 100 shares from another account and sell them. Your account gets credit for the cash, and you owe a debt: not a cash debt, but an obligation to pay back the stock you borrowed. In stock market lingo, you now have a *short position* in the stock.

A regular stock owner—someone with a *long* position—is hoping that the price of the stock will go up. When you're short, the opposite is true. If the price of the stock goes up, you'll have to pay more to buy the shares you need to repay your debt. You'll make money if the stock goes down, because then you can buy the stock cheaply and return the shares you sold earlier when the price was higher.

Example: When the price of XYZ is $35 you sell 100 shares short. Your brokerage account gets credit for $3,500. Later, you satisfy your obligation to return the 100 shares of XYZ by buying them at $32. You're left with a profit of $300, less brokerage commissions.

> When you have a short position, you're in exactly the opposite stance from someone who owns the stock. You make money when the stock goes down, and lose when it goes up.

Usual tax treatment. Generally speaking, you don't report any income or gain at the time you make a short sale. Even though you received money when you made the short sale, you don't know yet whether you're going to have a gain or loss. You find that out when you close the short sale by delivering the stock you owe. The cost of the stock you use to close the short sale determines whether you have a gain or a loss on the transaction. Limitations on this tax treatment are discussed below.

Short against the box. The strange thing about selling short is that you can do it even if you already own shares in that company. For example, if you own 100 shares of XYZ and want to sell 100, you can either sell the shares you own—or keep the shares you own and make a short sale. On Wall Street they call this going *short against the box.*

If you're short against the box, you've neutralized your market position. If the stock price goes up, the value of the shares you hold will increase, but the value of your short position will go down by the same amount. A similar cancellation occurs if the stock price goes down.

Selling short against the box would seem to be an ideal way to lock in your gains without paying tax:

Example: You have 1,000 shares of your company's stock from exercising a nonqualified option. The stock price has gone sky high since you exercised the option. If you sell the stock, you'll have to report a large gain. Worse, the gain will be short term because you exercised the option less than a year ago. You're worried that the stock price may be ready to dive.

Instead of selling the stock you own, you instruct your broker to make a short sale against the box. Because you've sold borrowed stock, instead of stock you own, you don't report gain or loss on the short sale. You have the cash from the sale, though, so you've locked in your gains from the stock. Later, you'll have a choice: you can close the short sale using the shares you already own, or buy new shares to close the short sale.

Unfortunately, as explained next, the tax law stands in the way of this elegant solution to your problem.

Limitations on using short sales

In an ideal world you would be able to use a short sale in this manner to protect the gain in your stock or options indefinitely while avoiding negative tax consequences. The tax law isn't that generous, however. Here are the main limitations on using this approach:

Immature ISO and ESPP stock. A short sale against the box should not be used to protect gains in stock from an incentive stock option or employee stock purchase plan before you've satisfied the special holding period. The IRS says this is a disqualifying disposition of the stock. That means you have to report compensation income at the time you make the short sale, even if you eventually use other stock to close the short sale.

Short-term holding period. If your stock has a short-term holding period when you make the short sale, its holding period will re-start when you close the short sale. As a result, the short sale may prevent you from using long-term capital gain rates when you eventually sell your stock.

> **Example:** You've held your stock for nine months, and the price has gone up substantially in that period of time. To protect your gain, you make a short sale against the box. Six months later you buy stock in the open market to close the short sale. You still own the original stock, and you've held it more than a year. Nevertheless, any gain from this stock will be short-term unless you hold it at least a year and a day beyond the date you closed the short sale.

This rule doesn't apply if the stock was already long-term at the time you entered into the short sale. In the example above, if you held the stock at least a year and a day before you made the short sale, any gain or loss on sale of the stock would be long-term. There's a rub, here, though. If you have a loss on the short sale, you'll have to treat that as a long-term loss. That may reduce the benefit of receiving a long-term gain from this stock or from other transactions.

Constructive sales. It gets worse. At one time it was possible to be short against the box for an indefinite period of time without having to report income or gain. The law now provides that you have to report a *constructive sale* of your stock if you're short against the box for an extended period of time. The rule applies only to *appreciated financial positions*—in other words, stock or options that would produce a gain if you sold them for fair market value.

To avoid a constructive sale, you need to close the short position by January 30 of the year after you established it, and continue to hold the long position (the stock) without a protective short position for at least 60 days. Otherwise you'll be treated as if you sold the original stock on the day you entered into the short sale.

> **Example:** You hold stock that has gone up in value since you bought it. In November, you make a short sale against the box. If you continue to hold the short position at the end of the following January, you'll have to report a sale of the stock in the year you made the short sale.
>
> To avoid this, you buy stock on the open market on January 20 and use this stock to close your short position. You continue to own the original shares. You'll still have to report a sale in the previous year if you establish a new short position in the following 60 days. If you bear the market risk of holding the stock *without* an offsetting short position for at least 60 days, you avoid having to report gain in the year of your short sale.

Using market options

Another possible way to protect your profits without selling your stock is to use *market options*—options you buy and sell through a broker. You can hedge against the risk of loss on your stock by buying a put option, or selling a call option—or both.

A *call option* is the same type of option you receive from your employer. It provides the holder with the right to purchase stock at a specified price. A *put option* provides the holder with the right to *sell* the stock at a specified price.

Example: You hold 1,000 shares of your company's stock, and they have gone up in value since you acquired them. You buy 10 put options (each put option applies to 100 shares) to sell at the current price. If the stock's price plummets, you can exercise the put option, forcing the person who sold the option to buy the stock at the favorable price that prevailed at the time you bought the option.

If the price goes up or stays the same, you won't exercise the put option. You'll lose the cost of the put option, but you won't complain because it acted as an insurance policy against the stock going down.

Selling a call option provides protection in a different way. You don't gain direct protection against the stock going down in value because you don't have a right to force a sale. But you've received a payment for the option (called the option *premium*), and that payment will at least partially offset any loss you have from a decline in the value of the stock. When you sell a call option, you give up the benefit of a future increase in the value of your stock, because the option will be exercised if the stock price goes up.

In some situations, people do *both*. They buy a put option and sell a call option at the same time. It may be possible to select options that have matching premiums: the amount you pay for the put option is the same as the amount you receive for selling the call option. In stock market lingo, this is a *costless collar*. It didn't cost you anything to put it in place, and it puts an upper and lower limit on your profit from the stock.

Unfortunately, these techniques invoke many complicated rules, and some of the issues don't have clear answers. The rules are so technical that you may have a hard time finding a tax professional who is well versed in them. What follows is the tip of the iceberg.

Immature ISO and ESPP stock. You shouldn't be considered to have made a disqualifying disposition of your immature stock from an incentive stock option or employee stock purchase plan if you buy a put option or sell a call option, provided that the market option isn't in the money at the time you do this. The contrary may be true if the option is in the money, or if you do *both* (buy a put and sell a call).

Short-term holding period. Here again you can end up with a short-term holding period even after you've held the stock more than a year. This is part of a very complicated set of rules called the *straddle rules*, and works much like the short sale rule described above.

Constructive sales. You can have a constructive sale as a result of option transactions, just as you can from a short sale against the box. You shouldn't have a constructive sale if you buy a put or sell a call when the market option isn't in the money. If the market option is in the money, or you use both techniques at once, you may have a constructive sale.

Loss deferral. If the combination of your stock holdings and your option position is a *straddle* under the tax rules, you can't claim a loss from one position if you have an unrecognized gain in the other position.

The straddle rules are quite complicated. They include rules under which you can avoid some of the negative consequences of holding a straddle if you sell *qualified covered calls*. Details on these rules are beyond the scope of this book.

Getting fancy

If your stock or options represent a great deal of wealth, your advisor may propose a sophisticated transaction with a fancy name: a zero-cost collar, or a variable forward sale, or perhaps a notional principal contract. These "financial products" have appropriate uses, and sometimes come into play in planning for equity compensation.

I suspect, though, that they're used in many situations where it would make more sense to sell the shares and pay the taxes.

One problem is that the tax savings you can legitimately claim from these strategies are usually not as large as they appear. You may end up merely deferring tax to a later year, and that can backfire if tax rates go higher. Another problem is the cost involved. These transactions tend to be quite expensive, and in some cases a significant part of the cost can be hidden.

> You may want to consider one of these strategies, but get a critical opinion before you move forward.

33

Estate Planning and Administration

Here are some things you should know about protecting your beneficiaries, or handling equity compensation in an estate.

THIS CHAPTER LOOKS AT THINGS YOU SHOULD DO to protect your heirs in case you die while holding options or another form of equity compensation, and offers some guidance for those faced with the task of dealing with these items after the owner has died.

While you're still with us

A complete discussion of estate planning is far beyond the scope of this book, but a few remarks are in order.

One purpose of estate planning is simply to make sure your assets go to the intended beneficiaries. You can do this through a last will and testament (perhaps supported by trust documents) or through beneficiary designations with respect to particular assets. If you leave assets that aren't covered by a will or beneficiary designation, they will pass according to state law, which won't necessarily conform to your wishes.

Another purpose of estate planning is to reduce costs and delays associated with disposition of your assets. A beneficiary designation may allow an asset to pass directly to that individual without being included among the assets that incur costs of probate. A trust may also be used to keep assets out of probate, or to reduce or eliminate estate tax.

> A good trusts and estates lawyer can guide you to a plan that's well suited to your situation and works under the laws of the state where you live. The result can be peace of mind for you and tremendous savings of time and money for your beneficiaries.

Keep up to date. Please, *please,* keep your beneficiary designations up to date. If your company provides a form for you to designate who gets your stock options or other items when you die, make sure it reflects your current situation. Imagine the mess if you die without having changed the designation you made to a spouse before a divorce, or to your first two children before a third one came along. This goes for your other designations, too, by the way: retirement plans, insurance policies, brokerage accounts and so forth.

The need for speed

Now we turn to some things you should know if you're a beneficiary or person responsible for handling an estate that includes stock options or other equity compensation. The first thing you need: information about options that might expire.

It's critically important to learn as quickly as possible the expiration dates of any options held by the decedent, and how those dates may be affected by his or her death. Options can be worth thousands of dollars—or *millions*—but they become entirely worthless when they expire. The company that issued the options is not under any obligation to help you figure out how to handle these assets or remind you to act before they expire. Furthermore, you may need to supply an original death certificate (not just a copy) and other documentation before you can exercise options held by the decedent, and those items aren't necessarily available at the snap of a finger.

> An option worth thousands or even millions of dollars can become completely worthless if you fail to act before it expires.

Options expire two different ways: at the normal expiration date, or after a specific event, including the death of the option holder. Most companies provide a year, or sometimes more than a year, after the death of the option holder for the estate or beneficiary to exercise the options. That's usually enough time to gather information, decide what to do, and obtain a death certificate and any other documentation that may be required.

You can't *assume* you'll have that much time, though. Companies aren't required to offer that much time, and some have chosen not to do so. Furthermore, the death of the option holder won't extend the normal expiration date. If an option holder dies two months before the date the option is set to expire, that's all the time you'll have to act, even if the company otherwise allows a full year. You may not feel like jumping into these issues right away, especially if you're dealing with grief at the loss of a loved one, but delay in getting this information can be costly.

You'll need other information of course, including the number of options, the type of options (nonqualified versus incentive stock option) and the exercise prices. First and foremost, though, focus on learning whether any valuable options may expire if you fail to act promptly.

Valuation of stock options

Stock options held by a decedent may contribute to the *taxable estate* that's used to determine the amount of estate tax, if any. The IRS issued guidance in 1998 (Revenue Procedure 98-34) saying that for estate tax purposes it would accept an option value that takes into account appropriate factors and uses a recognized valuation model, such as the Black-Scholes formula.

Income tax overview

An estate or beneficiary may have to pay income tax as a result of exercising an option or selling shares held by a decedent. The results are vastly different depending on the type of option.

A key part of the tax treatment is a basis adjustment that may apply to certain assets held by a decedent. The following discussion ignores a possible election to apply the adjustment six months after the date of death, and also ignores special rules that will apply only in 2010 as a result of the temporary repeal of the estate tax.

When it applies, the basis adjustment changes the tax basis of an asset to its value on the date of death. For example, if the decedent holds shares of stock bought for $40,000, but they are worth $75,000 on the date of death, the basis is changed to $75,000. A subsequent sale of those shares for $80,000 will require the estate or beneficiary to report only $5,000 of capital gain. The basis adjustment works in both directions, so if these shares had a value of $32,000 on the date of death the basis would be adjusted down to that number.

The basis adjustment doesn't apply to all assets held by a decedent, however. Generally speaking, it applies to items that would have been treated as capital gain or loss on the decedent's income tax return, but not to items that would have been ordinary income. We'll see that this rule provides favorable results for incentive stock options, somewhat less favorable results for stock from employee stock purchase plans, and unfavorable results for nonqualified stock options.

> Whenever the basis adjustment applies, the asset is treated as having a long-term holding period for purposes of the capital gain and loss rules, even if the decedent acquired the asset shortly before death and the estate or beneficiary sold the asset less than a year later.

Nonqualified stock options

Stock acquired by exercising a nonqualified stock option is treated like any other stock held by the decedent: its basis is adjusted to the date of death value, and its holding period is treated as long-term.

The options themselves *do not* receive a basis adjustment. The estate or beneficiary that exercises the option will have to report the bargain element of the option (the built in profit as of the date of exercise) as income. The shares will then have a basis equal to the amount paid to exercise the option increased by the amount of income reported—in other words, the basis will be equal to the value of the shares on the date of exercise.

This is essentially the same tax treatment that would have applied to the original option holder, but with two differences that should be noted. First, the income will be reported on Form 1099-MISC as income of the estate or beneficiary instead of appearing on the decedent's Form W-2. More importantly, if the option holder was an employee, social security and Medicare tax will be withheld *only if the option is exercised in the same year the option holder died.* As a result, delaying the option exercise until after the end of the year may produce tax savings, although other considerations may make earlier action more desirable.

Incentive stock options

The tax rules for incentive stock options held by a decedent are entirely different. Death eliminates the need to meet the special holding period for avoiding a disqualifying disposition. As a result, the basis adjustment applies to the option as well as the stock.

> Normally, an incentive stock option loses that status and converts to a nonqualified stock option three months after termination of employment. This rule does not apply after the death of the option holder, provided that the option qualified as an ISO at the time of death.

Treatment of stock. When someone dies after exercising an incentive stock option, but before selling or otherwise disposing of the shares, the shares can be sold at any time without causing a disqualifying disposition. The basis of the stock will be adjusted to the value on the date of death, so there will be no income tax on pre-death appreciation of the shares. Any gain or loss on a sale will be long-term, even if the shares are held less than a year.

> **Example:** An individual exercised an incentive stock option, paying $10,000 for shares worth $40,000, and died shortly thereafter while still holding the shares. On the date of death the shares were worth $45,000, so that became the new basis for the shares. In a subsequent sale of the shares for $48,000, the beneficiary pays tax on $3,000 of long-term capital gain.

Treatment of option. When someone dies holding an incentive stock option, a basis adjustment applies to the option itself. Normally an incentive stock option has no basis at all, but in this case the option acquires a basis equal to its value on the date of death. This has important implications for the estate or beneficiary when the option is exercised:

- The estate or beneficiary takes the basis of the option into account in determining the amount of AMT adjustment that applies upon exercise of the option. Note that this is important only if the estate or beneficiary holds the shares beyond the end of the year in which the option is exercised. Generally there is no reason to hold shares in this situation, because the holding period does not apply after the death of the original option recipient so an immediate sale will not be a disqualifying disposition.

- The estate or beneficiary also takes the basis of the option into account in determining the basis of the shares acquired by exercising the option. As a result, it may be possible to report little or no gain on the sale even though the option produced a sizeable profit.

Example: An incentive stock option had an exercise price of $12 and the stock was trading at $30 on the date its original recipient died. The value of the option, determined according to an option valuation model such as the Black-Scholes formula, was found to be $20 per share on the date of death, so this becomes the basis of the option. Several months later the estate exercised the option and sold the shares immediately at $35 per share.

The basis of the stock includes the basis of the option ($20 per share) plus the amount paid to exercise the option ($12 per share), so the stock had a basis of $32 per share. The estate reports a gain of $3 per share.

In the preceding example, the gain is short-term. The option itself acquired a long-term holding period because it was held by a decedent, but this holding period did not transfer to the shares acquired by exercise of the option.

Tax treatment of ESPP stock

The death of someone holding shares from an employee stock purchase plan results in a transfer of the shares, either to a beneficiary or to the estate. The transfer will not be treated as a disqualifying disposition, even if it occurs before the end of the normal holding period for these shares. However, if the ESPP provided a discount, even a qualifying transfer (one occurring after the end of the holding period) results in compensation income. As a result, the final return of the decedent will include compensation income measured the same way as if the decedent had satisfied the holding period and then sold the shares for an amount equal to the value of the shares on the date of death. See Chapter 27 for an explanation of how the taxable amount is determined. Note that this income appears on the decedent's return, not the return of the estate or beneficiary. The basis of the shares in the hands of the estate or beneficiary will simply be the value of the shares on the date of death.

34

Medicare Tax on Investment Income

Beginning in 2013, high-income individuals are required to
pay Medicare tax on net investment income.

THE AFFORDABLE CARE ACT—the healthcare reform perhaps
better known as Obamacare—imposes some new taxes. One is a
Medicare tax on net investment income, which includes (among
other items) dividends and capital gains. The tax applies only if your
overall income is above a threshold amount.

What you'll pay

This tax is in addition to any other tax you owe for the year (such
as regular income tax and alternative minimum tax), and applies at
the rate of 3.8%. For every $1,000 of income to which it applies, you'll
pay an additional $38.

Not absorbed by AMT credit. If you've exercised incentive stock options and held shares for qualifying sales, you may be eligible to claim AMT credit to the extent your regular income tax exceeds your tax as calculated under AMT rules. The Medicare tax on net investment income is not part of the regular income tax, so it doesn't figure into this calculation. AMT credit cannot be used to offset this tax.

Taxable amount

The tax is imposed on your *net investment income*, but only to the extent your overall income exceeds a threshold that depends on your filing status: $250,000 when married filing jointly or a qualifying widow(er); $125,000 when married filing separately; otherwise $200,000. These amounts are not indexed for inflation. Here are some examples:

Example 1: You're single and your income consists of $100,000 in wages and $50,000 in investment income. Because your overall income is below the threshold for a single filer, your taxable amount is zero and you do not pay Medicare tax on your investment income.

Example 2: You're single and have $180,000 in wages together with $50,000 in investment income. Your overall income exceeds the $200,000 threshold by $30,000. That's less than your investment income for the year, so your taxable amount is $30,000. You pay 3.8% Medicare tax on that amount, in addition to regular income tax and, if applicable, AMT.

Example 3: You're single and have $240,000 in wages plus $50,000 in investment income. Now your overall income of $290,000 exceeds the threshold by $90,000, but you pay this 3.8% additional tax only on the $50,000 of investment income.

Net investment income

For purposes of this tax, net investment income includes most items we would normally think of as investment income, such as interest, dividends and capital gains. Exempt interest on bonds issued by state and local governments escapes the tax. Investment earnings within a 401k, IRA, or other qualified retirement account are not included, and distributions from these accounts are not treated as investment income.

Overall income

Overall income for most people is simply adjusted gross income. This figure takes into account certain specified deductions, such as contributions to IRAs, but not the deduction for personal exemptions, the standard deduction, or itemized deductions (such as deductions for home mortgage interest or state and local taxes). If you worked outside the United States and used the foreign earned income exclusion, you have to add back the amount you excluded.

Note that although distributions from retirement accounts are not treated as investment income, they can increase your overall income, moving investment income above the threshold.

> **Example:** You're married filing jointly and have $200,000 of wages and $30,000 of capital gain. Without more, you do not pay Medicare tax on investment income because your overall income is below the $250,000 threshold for joint filers. If you also have $40,000 of income from a retirement plan distribution, your overall income is $270,000 and you pay Medicare tax on $20,000 of your capital gain.

Planning for equity compensation

Most types of equity compensation are not directly affected by this tax. Shares you hold after receiving them may produce dividend income or capital gain that could be subject to the tax if your overall income is high enough, but the same is true if you sell these shares and reinvest the proceeds in some other stock.

You need to be aware of this tax, though, if you exercise an incentive stock option. Holding shares can convert ordinary income to long-term capital gain. This can be an advantage even when Medicare tax applies to the capital gain, because the rate on ordinary income is higher even when the Medicare tax is added to the capital gain rate.

This is not the case, however, if you are in a situation where AMT deprives you of the benefit of converting ordinary income to capital gain. As explained in Chapter 18 under the heading *Unrecovered Credit*, you may reach a point where holding additional ISO shares produces no benefit apart from increasing the amount of AMT credit that carries over to future years. Although conversion of the income to capital gain produces no benefit, you incur Medicare tax on the capital gain. In this situation, it is possible to pay *more* tax on capital gain than you would on ordinary income from a disqualifying disposition.

Resources

Taxation of Stock Transactions

Capital Gains, Minimal Taxes: The Essential Guide for Investors and Traders by Kaye A. Thomas (Fairmark Press Inc.). A plain language explanation of tax rules that apply to people who buy and sell stocks, mutual funds and stock options, and strategies for minimizing those taxes. For details and ordering information:

www.fairmark.com/books/cgmt.htm

Web Sites for Option Holders

Fairmark.com. This site offers an online tax guide for investors, which includes additional information on many of the topics covered in this book. You'll find a section where we post updates, corrections and clarifications to this book, and a message board where you can post comments and ask questions.

myStockOptions.com. This web site has a wealth of materials dealing with stock options and related subjects.

Web Sites for Companies and Administrators

Certified Equity Professional Institute (cepi.scu.edu). This unit of Santa Clara University provides training and a certification exam for people who manage or administer stock option plans for companies.

National Association of Stock Plan Professionals (naspp.com). This membership association provides resources on stock compensation through regularly scheduled webcasts, a bi-monthly newsletter, educational programs, the NASPP Blog, and the NASPP Annual

Conference. The NASPP also publishes the most extensive survey on stock plan design and has over 30 regional chapters.

National Center for Employee Ownership (nceo.org). A membership organization that focuses on ways to provide equity ownership to employees. NCEO publishes some of the leading books on stock options and holds meetings and seminars.

Index

also from Fairmark Press:

Equity Compensation Strategies
A guide for professional advisors

This book for financial advisors and other professionals explains how to formulate, evaluate and implement sound strategies for handling stock options and other forms of equity compensation.

Capital Gains, Minimal Taxes
The essential guide for investors and traders

This plain language book makes it easy to understand the rules—and the best strategies for minimizing taxes. It's your complete, authoritative guide to taxation of stocks, mutual funds and market-traded stock options.

Go Roth!
Your guide to the Roth IRA, Roth 401k & Roth 403b

Learn how to get the most from a Roth retirement account. This book covers everything from the basics of choosing a Roth IRA and setting it up to the strategies that will help you build and preserve wealth.

That Thing Rich People Do
Required reading for investors

A short, readable book that explains all the key principles of investing.

Made in the USA
San Bernardino, CA
20 September 2017